From the Other Side of the Bench

Hon. Peter M. Leavitt

ISBN: 10:1502367246
ISBN: 13: 9781502367242

Praise for *From the Other Side of the Bench*

"In this book, you'll read about a man who began his career as a stand-up comic and ended up as one of the most respected criminal and civil court judges in New York State. You'll learn about the time he was called as a witness in a murder trial because he was also the responding Emergency Medical Technician tending to the victim. You'll also learn what it was like to be the trial judge for an infamous, racially charged murder case, where a white off-duty policeman shot and killed a black motorist in a fight over a parking space. You'll read about the author's immigrant family and how their love, humor, ethics, loyalty, and feistiness shaped who he is today.

"Judge Leavitt has had fourteen of his noteworthy civil and criminal law decisions published, and a forty-plus-year legal career handling cases from the mundane (disorderly conduct and speeding tickets) to the severe (rape and murder). He discusses these and many more intriguing trials and experiences. He also provides insights regarding celebrity justice, drugs, the jury system, and more.

"In reviewing this book, I am reminded of the many ways Judge Leavitt inspired me to become an attorney. His love of the law and more importantly his love for people are the hallmarks of his life and service to the bench. I shall always be grateful for knowing Judge Leavitt."

—Salvatore Lagonia, former police officer in the town of New Castle, now a practicing attorney

"There have been numerous books written about the law and the court system, but few written by someone with as unique a perspective as Judge Leavitt. The book chronicles his transition from the stage to the bench, the emotional juggernaut of being a judge, the tears and tragedies and his constant and enduring love of the law.

Right out of high school, he was recruited by the USO as a comedian, but as much as he loved the stage he discovered that he could not make a living in show business. His subsequent life-changing decision to go to college and law school was made partly with the ulterior motive that if he became a trial attorney, he would still have a stage and a microphone. That perfectly describes the Judge Leavitt I know."

—Peter Tartaglia, private investigator for over twenty-five years, licensed and bonded by the Department of State, Associated Licensed Detectives of New York State, and the National Council of Investigative Specialists; personal bodyguard; trainer for police and correction officers.

"After graduating from Fordham Law School, Judge Leavitt became an assistant district attorney in Brooklyn, New York. That job culminated in his becoming a Supreme Court trial assistant. Judge Leavitt then became an assistant district attorney in Westchester County, New York.

"Due to a growing family with a wife and two daughters, Judge Leavitt then went into private practice as a defense and trial attorney in Chappaqua, New York, practicing there for eighteen years with his practice moving into civil law as well. Seeking the ability to have a wider influence in the courts, he ran for and was elected town justice and served in that capacity for ten years. Judge Leavitt ran for and was elected to Westchester County Court. He was appointed as a New York State acting Supreme Court justice, and served in that capacity for eight years. Judge Leavitt pulls no punches and his criticisms provide an astute analysis of people and institutions that deserve a little more scrutiny than they generally receive.

"Having spent years on all three sides of the courtroom—prosecutor, defense attorney, and trial judge—Judge Peter Leavitt now shares decades of insights, laced with both hard-hitting analysis and poignant personal stories. Through this 'semi-autobiographical' book, Judge Leavitt demystifies the court system—and the men and women on both sides of the bench as few have done before him."

—Brian Stone, former assistant district attorney in the Rackets Bureau Suffolk County, New York; former special assistant attorney general in the Office of the Special Prosecutor for Corruption in New York City; former assistant attorney general in the New York State Organized Crime Task Force Office.

From the Other Side of the Bench

Murder, Mafia, Marijuana, the Media, and the Man

A somewhat autobiographical book by The Honorable Peter M. Leavitt

TABLE OF CONTENTS

Acknowledgments xiii

Introduction xv

Chapter 1: Growing Up in Brooklyn 1

Chapter 2: My Extended Family 11

Chapter 3: But Seriously, Folks...My Career as a Stand-Up Comic 18

Chapter 4: Riding Homicide: Twenty-Four Hours of Hands-On Horror 24

Chapter 5: The Woman Behind the Man 32

Chapter 6: The Prosecution of Frank Sacco 37

Chapter 7: The Wisdom of a Lower Court Judge 45

Chapter 8: My Election: Let's Get On with It and Open the Bubbly! 55

Chapter 9: Court Officers: "You Have to Be On the Job 15 Years to Know" 65

Chapter 10: The Nature of Evidence: "I Did Not Know You Could Do That!" 71

Chapter 11: A History of Juries: "Not to Accuse an Innocent Man or Spare a Guilty One" 85

Chapter 12: Juries Today: "The Jury's Responsibility Is to Deliver Justice" 90

Chapter 13: Jury Selection: Strategies and Stereotypes 104

Chapter 14: How Much Justice Can You Afford? 107

Chapter 15: Court and TV: "We All Pay the Price" 111

Chapter 16: The Courts and Big Business 117

Chapter 17: The Judge's Team 124

Chapter 18: The Roots of Law 135

Chapter 19: Threats: "I Still Look Behind Me" 142

Chapter 20: Witnesses: Being "Too Credible" 144

Chapter 21: Addictions: "Five Manhattans for Lunch and Nothing to Eat!" 153

Chapter 22: Children and Crime: "Hi, Judge. You Did Me a Favor. Thank You." 158

Chapter 23: Anatomy of a Trial 169

Chapter 24: Practicing Law: "You're from *the City*, Aren't You?" 190

Chapter 25: Making Unpopular Decisions 198

Chapter 26: Halting the Abuse of Power 208

Chapter 27: Bonnie Briar Syndicate vs. the Town of Mamaroneck 211

Chapter 28: Good-Byes...213

Chapter 29: Closing Arguments 218

About the Author...221

Acknowledgments

I wish to thank the following people for the considerable help and advice that they have given me in writing this book:

- My daughters, Karen Leavitt and Amy Gramlich, for giving me their editorial advice and love and support, and for refreshing my memory on a constant basis.
- Roberta "Bobbie" Eden, for her gentle persuasion, which finally got me to sit down and start writing this book. For her unending patience in letting me read large portions to her more than once! For always loving me.
- Bill Rosvally, for teaching me so much about the law whenever I had a new or unique challenge, and for giving me advice on an ongoing basis.
- "Mookie," who spent years teaching me how a courtroom should be run.
- Carl Vergari, the former district attorney, who took a chance on me.
- My friend Jack Abramowitz, who serves as my sounding board.
- My editor, Chris Finer, without whose help and insightful comments this book would be somewhat disjointed.
- My computer guru, my daughter Karen, who keeps the keys working, and my cardiologist, who keeps me working. Cannot leave out my Keurig and my microwave.

Introduction

I do not remember how long I have wished to write a book. I only know how hard it has been to finally sit down and start. I have been a lecturer, professor, and entertainer for over a quarter of a century, as well as a lawyer for over forty years and a judge for eighteen. My students and audiences often tell me how much they enjoy – and learn from – my anecdotes. But I do not want to just tell you stories. I want to tell you about my experiences and the family who shaped me—and tell this to you in my best storytelling manner.

I don't expect to be on any best-seller lists or to win any awards, especially after you read about how I feel about the media, poorly prepared attorneys, insurance companies, a small percentage of bad judges and police, and the media (I dislike them twice as much as any other group.) I do, however, hope that you will take something away from this book—something about the way the lives we live and the people we become shape our decision-making. When it's your *job* to make decisions, decisions that lead to life-altering consequences, understanding how and why judges—or *this* judge, anyway—reach their decisions can, I hope, be both instructive and entertaining.

Or perhaps I am just a storyteller after all, and this book is just for me.

1

Growing Up in Brooklyn

I was born in April of 1938, in Brooklyn, New York, and it was a magical place for a child. My father was an attorney, and we were what in those days was called *comfortable.* Following the Depression my dad had made enough money to help his brothers financially, putting the youngest, Alex, through medical school. He leant money to his brothers-in-law Sam and Mosey in their respective businesses, put my sister through college, and helped my brother and me through college and law school. In addition, we owned two homes and my parents traveled all over the world.

By the time we were older and could be left alone, Mom would go to my Dad's office to help out as a secretary. She knew shorthand and could type. She decided that when my dad would call out in his law office for her to come in and take dictation, it would sound unprofessional for a client to hear him call out "Jenny!" Her name was Jeannette and her middle initial was G., so she chose to be called JG. My brother Dik (his chosen nickname, really Richard) was six years older than I, and my sister Lenore—Lonni, as she was known to all—was six years younger.

I was too young to know what that German monster was up to in Europe, but during World War Two, I started, just barely, to understand what was occurring. When I was five years old, I would see my mother start to cry after Dad would come home and report the day's news. I don't remember any specifics of those somber reports. Perhaps our parents thought it better that we didn't know.

But there were those times that relatives or close friends would come over to our house. They would go into the sun parlor and close the door so the three of us could not hear them talk about the war, but Dik would tell us what he'd heard. The only actual memory I have of what Dik told us was that millions of Jewish people were being killed. I do remember that the day the war ended everyone was very happy, but still very cautious about what had happened. I might have been too young to really understand that my people were being annihilated, but I knew it was making everyone sad and scared. My mother would never answer any questions about members of her family who were still in Hungary—or that we'd *thought* were still in Hungary.

I've since learned that not one had survived. Of her entire family, only my mother, Grandmother Minnie, and my Aunt Elsie were alive. I remember that my father sat the three of us down one night after the war and cautioned us, "Be careful what you say to strangers whenever anyone you don't know talks about Jews." The fear was planted early, and caution has remained with me.

We lived in a two-family house in the Flatbush section of Brooklyn called Midwood that my father bought from a bank after the Wall Street crash. The ground floor had three bedrooms. A front door led into a small vestibule—on the left you were led to the dining room, the living room to the right of that, and the sun parlor to the right of that. A left through the dining room brought you to the kitchen on the left and a bedroom on the right. The bathroom was next on the left. (Can you imagine one bathroom for a family of five?! Somehow we made do.) Lonni's small bedroom was the one on the right. Finally, there were two rear bedrooms—boys on one side and parents on the other. A wide driveway led to a huge backyard that was all concrete and had a two-car garage. It was big enough to build half a basketball court outside the garage, and a stickball court inside when both cars were not parked there—we regularly used the garage's back wall as "home plate" and the strike zone was a rectangular box that we had painted on the wall.

My childhood was filled with games. We played stickball with a broomstick and a Spalding ball. We played stoopball on our front steps and Mumbly-Peg and marbles on a little patch of ground on the side of the house. We played Skully, a game in which we'd fill a bottle cap with wax and flick it on a chalk playing field drawn on the street. We traded comics and baseball cards, and I still have not forgiven myself for trading away my Duke Snider card, which I replaced years later for a lot more money than the original cost me.

We played cops and robbers using Gene Autry, Tom Mix, or Roy Rogers cap pistols, and Cowboys and Indians, and yes, while you could get shot and "killed," this was the extent of our violent games. We sometimes played on the roofs of the apartment houses on Ocean Avenue. We played hide-and-seek, tag, thumb war, and lots of basketball. We took marathon bike rides and played Ringolevio, Dodgeball, Kick the Can, Red Rover, Red Light-Green Light, a hopscotch-like game called Potsie, and others that have faded from my memory. We played in the street and in our backyards, and we always felt safe.

We took trips to Riis Park, Nathan's in Coney Island with all the rides and games, the Paramount Theatre, the Brooklyn Museum, the Bronx Zoo, and Ebbets Field, where we'd go to see "Dem Bums," the Brooklyn Dodgers. (They were "bums" until they won the World Series in 1955 and stayed our heroes until they left Brooklyn, when a long period of mourning began.)

One year, I worked all summer to buy my first three-speed bike. I treasured that bike and would have brought it into the house every night if my parents had let me. The bike was my ticket to explore the world beyond East 22nd Street in Brooklyn. I could go almost anywhere as long as I had done my homework and was home in time for dinner. That first summer, I used it to make deliveries for the local butcher after school and for the hardware store the following summer.

I had to leave my bike at home and take the subway to Coney Island for my next summer job with one of my father's clients: Nat Faber's Fascination, Pokerino, Skeeball and Penny Arcade, right near the Cyclone roller coaster. It became my favorite job for the next few years. After several summers, I became a "carnie" and knew everyone at all the rides and games. I never had to pay for a ride and I would shill for the games. I took many dates there years later, and when all those vendors and pitchmen greeted me by name; the girls were so impressed!

My role model growing up was my big brother Dik. He was tall and smart and athletic and very popular. He was good at all sports and taught me with a quiet patience. He served as my entry into my high school service fraternity. Our Chapter was named A.Z.A. Kolbert, named after a WW2 veteran. Dik was my confidant, and I would pester him into taking me with him when he went driving or out with his friends. I loved to spend time with him.

Dik was brilliant. He graduated with many honors, including one from Columbia Law School. That said, attending the same grammar school and high school as he did caused me innumerable traumas. Teachers would invariably ask, "Are you sure you are Richard's brother? He was so smart! What happened to you?" At the time I hated all the attention I received because of him and wanted to change my name. I got over it.

While Dik was my role model, my mother was my soul. Mom was a fiery Hungarian and everyone loved her (except two of my father's sisters, known within the family as "Arsenic" and "Old Lace"). But Mom never got rattled. She was always there with a calm voice when she needed to iron out the wrinkles among us. She had a temper when it came to anyone outside the family, though, especially someone who had insulted or hurt one of us. She had a keen eye in the marketplace and always managed to save money, both because she wanted to and because her memories of the Depression were so vivid.

We had many dogs over the years, and every dog had its tale. Her favorite stories were about Coke, whom she'd found in an alley as a pup. Some cruel person had bent a wire around his tail, so she set it with wooden Good Humor sticks and adhesive tape. Coke was malnourished and scared. She wrapped him in a towel and took him home. He was pitch black, which is why we named him Coke—after the coal, not the soda. He was in our family for over fifteen years. He was a mutt, part German shepherd and part con man. He sired many litters in the neighborhood to the absolute dismay of the other dogs' owners. He was a true member of the family: he loved my mom and loved the rest of us, but she was his favorite.

As a result of the rationing during the war, my mother had to really work at feeding us well. Of course, that was at a time when we ate all the things we've since learned were bad for us: red meat, chicken fat, and so forth. I have never been obese, but I was what my mom would refer to as "healthy." She was a creative cook who hated to waste anything. "Children in Europe are starving," she'd frequently remind us. This meant that you had to eat whatever was on your plate, but that wasn't difficult because she was such a good cook.

I have many wonderful memories of food. It seems that Mom and I spent a lot of time together in the kitchen because she thought I would make a good sous-chef, and we always had fun. Each week, our greengrocer, Mr. Klerman, would drive down the street and would always stop in for a *cuppa* and a *nosh*. He always pinched my cheek (I hated that) and gave me an apple. Then he would sit and spend a long time dishing out the neighborhood gossip with my mother.

I would listen but not understand their winks, their nods, their unspoken meanings. My mother would give him her order for the week, and he would go to his truck and make it up. My job was very important: I was to go out with him and watch out for Mr. Klerman putting his thumb on the scale when he was weighing the produce. I don't think he really wanted to cheat us, but old habits die hard following the bad years of the Depression and the war.

I remember with such fondness walking with my mom to the store. Since I helped her shop, she would get me a treat like a Charlotte Russe, all pound cake and whipped cream with a cherry on top all packed inside a white cardboard cylinder, or a chocolate egg cream, which contained no egg and no cream, just a little seltzer (two cents plain) in a glass with some chocolate syrup and milk. Heaven!

One weekend on a visit home from college, Dik brought a dozen Dunkin' Donuts. Mom rationed them closely, of course, and by Day 3, they were as hard as sugary stones. Suddenly, they disappeared. That Sunday after dinner, my mother served dessert: vanilla pudding! I loved vanilla pudding. We all dug in—and found those donuts on the bottom of the dish. Mom explained that she'd been sure the pudding would soften them enough to eat and wouldn't you know it – she was right. Dik told that story for years. Whenever I needed to make him laugh I only had to look at him and say, "Pudding and surprise!"

There were a few errors that took place in the kitchen over the years. Once, my mother was making matzo balls for chicken soup for the holidays using a pound of English flour a client had given my dad as a gift. My mother thought it would make a nice, expensive matzo ball treat, but it was too different from American flour. The matzo balls that year were so hard that we could have used them for doorstops.

My father would delight in putting my mother's cooking skills to the test every so often. We had company over for dinner on a regular basis, mostly Dad's family and my parents' close friends. Dad would come home and proclaim, "Jenny, I have some new clients I invited over for dinner next Saturday night. They are world travelers and so you have to come up with something new and different, not your famous chicken paprika or your brisket—which are to die for!—but something *new*!"

Thus the challenge was made, and my mom would sit with me the next day and ask if I had any ideas. After tossing out fish and beef as insufficiently new or different, she would light up and say she had an idea. "What?" I would ask, and she would say she was still writing the recipe in her head. On one such occasion, we went to the butcher and she ordered six squabs, though she had never before made squab.

When Mr. Klerman came the next day, she bought six pineapples from him. My job was to carefully remove the top of the pineapples and scoop out the inside, which I was free to nosh on. She made a lovely salad, cooked the squabs, put them inside the pineapples, cooked them in the oven for a short time, and served them with wild rice and asparagus with hollandaise sauce. I've been to many fine and fancy restaurants, and I've been to cooking school, but that was still the finest meal I have ever had.

It was impossible to buy presents for my mom. We would start to ask her way before her birthday what she would like.

She always had the same answer: "You are enough for me; I have everything I want." We would nag and pester her and she would respond, "I don't want perfume; it gives me a headache. I don't want clothing; I make my own or I'll keep repairing what I have. I don't want jewelry; since your father never takes me anyplace that I would wear it!" That last comment was made tongue in cheek. She never, ever had a bad word to say about my dad.

But there *was* one time I bought her a great gift for her birthday. We had rented a house on Lake Oscawana in Upstate New York. I must have been twenty-one or so, and I was driving in the country that day, trying to come up with something more interesting and memorable than simply taking her out for dinner. I drove past a farm and saw a very, *very* old horse with a sway-back, a back so swayed that his stomach nearly brushed the ground. I drove into the farm and spoke to the farmer, who told me he was going to sell the horse for twenty-five dollars for glue. I was probably a little gullible but I believed him. I bought the horse, and together we proceeded to put him into the back of my 1949 Buick convertible by removing the back seat.

He pushed and I pulled, but the horse had no intention of getting into that car! The more we worked the more we laughed, and the more stubborn the horse became. We finally bribed him into the car with a carrot and a little gentle persuasion from the rear. I drove home at ten miles an hour with that poor terrified horse neighing all the way.

When I pulled up in front of the house, my mom, Aunt Elsie, and two friends were playing canasta on the deck. My mom had her back to the road. Aunt Elsie said, "Jennie, don't look now, but I think Peter has just brought home your birthday present!" Her laughter was worth all those years of torment, of not knowing what to get her for a present. She drove back with me to the farm and paid the farmer one hundred dollars to help me get the confused horse *back out* of the car and for his promise to put the horse out to pasture and forget about the glue factory.

So, I've told you that my mother was my soul and my brother Dik was my role model. My father was my conscience. He had a wonderful ethic in bringing up the three of us. He let us know very early in life, "I will house you, feed you, clothe you and educate you. But if you want anything else, get a part-time job after school and in the summers to earn your own money!" It was by following this advice that I was able to buy that bicycle and it was also how Dik bought his first car.

My dad had a law practice in Downtown Brooklyn, where he specialized in real estate law but worked as a general practitioner. This meant that he would do any kind of civil law, including matrimonial, but not criminal law. For whatever reason, in whatever season, when I had time off from school my dad would take me with him to Court Street—16 Court Street, a giant anthill of attorneys and accountants.

I remember that every once in a while my dad would let me sit in his office on the big leather couch in the back of the room while he was advising a client. I learned what to ask and how to listen and how to counsel. I learned more psychology in that office than in all the psychology courses I took in college. He would quietly listen to clients, and then he would ask questions that invariably would lead them to their own solutions.

He could make clients feel good about whatever answers they'd come up with. He would let them cry when it was appropriate, laugh at themselves when needed, and generally they would depart with a smile and a big thank-you to him. I don't glorify and I don't embellish. Everyone who knew my dad knew that he was a very wise and professional lawyer.

On the weekends, Dad usually had a place to go or a client to visit. He would alternate who he'd take with him. He seemed to enjoy giving each of us some one-on-one time, and I was always overjoyed when he picked me. There was always a lesson to learn wherever we went or whomever we saw. When I was mature enough to ask, he would explain what had happened during the Depression. He talked about our neighbors who made do with whatever they could and our hated next-door neighbor who had dealt rationed sugar and meat on the black market.

He had no patience for people who cheated or lied. The worst thing you could do as a child in my family was lie. Even if you had done something really bad, if you told him the truth he would work it out so that your punishment was fair and just. On the other hand, if you lied he could be very intimidating, so I learned early on to level with him. From my father I learned to *insist* on the truth, a trait that stayed with me throughout my life, especially when I was sitting on the bench.

My dad had a keen eye for people with intelligence and potential. He helped start people in business, people who became very rich and who took him along as their attorney and sometimes as a partner. He didn't always guess right, but did more often than not. He had one client, Patsy Mootsie, whose dream was to open a luncheonette and pizza store.

My dad helped him out by lending him money and doing all his legal work. He didn't ask Patsy for anything. We would go to his store and have pizza every month or so, just Dad and me, and once, on the way home, I asked my dad if he ever thought he would get the loan paid back. He told me that he was sure that he would, if we could just manage to eat enough pizza.

My dad was my conscience. I have lived all my life hearing his gentle voice, even after he passed away, urging me along the path he believed in. He was a wonderful man and had strength for all of his family, immediate and extended. He always had time to listen and then to help you make the right decision.

2

My Extended Family

My mother had a sister, Elsie, and their mother was Nana, a wonderfully warm and huggable grandmother, always ready with a huge smile whenever she saw me. Her name was Minnie, and she was devoted to Pop (her husband Harry and the only grandfather I ever knew). My father's father died before I was born, my mother's father died when Mom was very young, and Minnie married Pop years later.

Minnie was a funny lady. She always had her hair and makeup done just right and she just made you feel good being with her. She could listen to you forever and make you feel that whatever you had to say was important. Minnie used an expression that my family has repeated thousands of times since she uttered it. We were walking on Kings Highway in Brooklyn with Minnie and Pop, going to a restaurant, and a woman was walking on the other side of the street wearing the most outrageous hat. I do not recall if it was the hat's hideous color, its tremendous size, or the fact that it had animal parts attached to it. But I do remember that Minnie, this gentle, white-haired grandmother of mine, looked at the woman and whispered to us, "The things you see when you haven't got a gun!" That was my Nana.

Speaking of guns, I haven't told you anything about the army, which I enlisted in when I was 18. The most vivid memory I have was both a terrible and eye-opening learning experience for me. After my basic training, I was stationed at Fort Leavenworth, Kansas. I flew to Kansas City, Missouri, and remember being able to see all the way to Leavenworth. Okay, that's a bit of an exaggeration, but Missouri is a very flat state. I reported to my barracks early on a Sunday and checked in with the duty sergeant who assigned me to my quarters on the second floor. I proceeded upstairs and began to unpack my uniforms and toiletries. The place was deserted on Sunday and it was nice and quiet. A few moments passed and a corporal walked into the room. I cannot describe him as a redneck. This huge brute had *no* neck. He sat down without saying hi or any other greeting. I nodded to him when he came in, and he proceeded to watch me hang up my clothes and put my stuff in my footlocker. Less than five minutes elapsed when he said to me, "YOU A JEW?"

I had few choices since I figured that he had already seen my 201 file, which I had given to the duty sergeant. It tells your religion and anything else the army knows about you. Since I wanted to avoid having this brute pummel me, I answered truthfully, "Yes, I am." More time passed and he then said, "YOU A LIAR?"

"Why would I lie to you?" was my snappy rebuttal.

He said, "BOTH YOU MAMMY AND PAPPY JEWS?" I said yes.

"IF YOU ALL JEW, WHERE ARE YOUR HORNS?"

His remark floored me for an instant. Because I am from Brooklyn, and Jewish, and because his IQ was probably under fifty, I avoided a physical attack by telling him with a straight face, "We have them surgically removed at birth." He seemed to be mollified and left. Sad comment, but I thought it better that I keep the incident to myself rather than report this creature. After all, he was just a product of his environment. I have experienced numerous instances of Anti-Semitism happen during my lifetime, and often it is hard to hold your anger back since you want to tell people:

1. I did not kill Christ,
2. I am not a moneylender,
3. I do not control Hollywood and the media.

As I got older, I would continue to innocently ask Mom about her family, aunts, uncles, and cousins, but she would get teary and hug me very hard and I would know to stop asking. I was her favorite, or so she would tell anyone who would listen, and sadly these words were sometimes uttered in front of both my brother Dik and sister Lonni. Many years passed before I came to understand Mom's need to hold me so close, when I learned that I'd had another brother, Barry, born between Dik and me, who died when he was sixteen months old.

"Arsenic" and "Old Lace" were Fannie and Sarah, two of my father's sisters, and they were impossible to my mother, treating her like an indentured servant when they descended every summer – not at the same time, but one after the other as perpetual houseguests. Knowing that she could sew, they would drop off clothing to repair and give her a date by which to have it ready. They would invite themselves to dinner, never thinking to bring a little gift, and always asking to take the leftovers home.

Old Lace and Arsenic not only despised my mother; they hated each other so much that they would never be in our house together. They'd stopped talking to each other over twenty years earlier. But they both liked me and both agreed to both come to my wedding. Chaos! Of course I insisted they be seated at the same table, perhaps out of gleeful spite for the abuse they had heaped on my Mom over the years. After some forced pleasantries and a glass or two of wine, they began talking and could not remember what they had fought about or why they had stopped talking.

I loved my mom's mother and stepfather. I really adored Pop and Nana. He was English, and he'd apprenticed in England and Italy as a fine cabinetmaker. He later opened a shop specializing in custom furniture in New York, and was very successful. In fact, Milton Berle hired him to design and make furniture for his mother. He had a very old wooden workbench that dated from the 1800s that he had brought over from Europe. After Pop retired, my parents brought his entire workshop to our house, and in a very large finished basement with old casement windows, they set Pop up with all his tools and veneers and glues. When Pop died, he left me all his tools and the workbench. I still have and use the workbench almost every day.

When I came home from high school, Pop would let me watch him build something. I watched a long time before he finally began to teach me his craft. My first project was a doorstop. No, it was not insulting, just his way of watching every move I made, my measuring skills, my use of the wood saw, my sandpapering and varnishing. I am happy to this day that I spent so much quality time with him. Pop never used a power tool—I learned to use saws, chisels, wood planes, mallets, screwdrivers, pliers—and a lot of sandpaper. We talked and worked for hours each day and cleaned up together before dinner. Each night I would drive with Dad to take him home if he wasn't staying with us to eat.

My mom's sister Elsie was, according to my mother, one of Eleanor Roosevelt's correspondence secretaries. She—Aunt Elsie, not Eleanor Roosevelt—was very quiet and very talented. When we would go to the Bronx to visit Aunt Elsie and Uncle Jack, my mother would bring her violin and Elsie would play the piano, and Elsie's husband Jack would sit there with a giant smile on his face. Jack thought that he was the luckiest man alive to have married Elsie. He owned his own barbershop and was as sweet a man as a boy could want for an uncle. When Jack died too young, of a massive coronary, Elsie totally collapsed, had a nervous breakdown, and spent the rest of her life in Pilgrim State Hospital. I used to drive my mom out to the hospital on Long Island to visit, and she always cried all the way home.

While it sounds as if I loved my mom's family more than my dad's—and I must admit it was harder to feel warm fuzzies toward Dad's family than my mom's—I loved and admired my dad's brother Moses. Uncle Moe was great. He was always serious, very loving, and a giant of a man. He was also a famous guy. He was part of the JDC, the Joint Distribution Committee. He met with kings and presidents before and after World War II to work on the resettlement of the Jewish people scattered all over the world. I went to Israel this past spring; I was on a quest to see the library named after him at Hebrew University. When I arrived, I was met by the dean of the school and personally escorted to the library. The first rooms were new and so was the huge sign honoring my Uncle Moe, but when we went to a different section, there was the sign that I recognized from a picture in the family album. Fifty years ago my parents had gone there, and Dad had taken a picture of that very sign. Remembering those times fills me with emotion and upon seeing that very same sign, I shed not just a few tears.

I was also crazy about my dad's brother-in-law, Arsenic's husband, Uncle Mosey. He owned a mattress store, and Dik and I loved to go to the balcony and jump down onto a pile of mattresses. He didn't mind but would warn us not to hurt ourselves. I also loved Old Lace's husband, Uncle Sam. We would play cards, and he taught me how to play pinochle. Then there were those wonderful people, easy-going and relaxed, Uncle Ben and Dad's sister Aunt Tillie who moved to Columbus, Ohio, probably to get away from Tillie's sisters. Ben was a mathematics whiz and would always have trick questions for me. I also had a very close relationship with Dad's brother Philip and Philip's wife Ruth. They had two famous daughters: Wendy Drew, who was a soap opera personality on the radio, and the renowned Allegra Kent, the ballerina.

Now that I am writing this, I'm realizing that it was only Arsenic and Old Lace I disliked. I had a fine relationship with my dad's brother Alex, who was a doctor. Alex served in France during World War Two in a MASH unit near the front lines. He never talked about the serious parts of the war, or anything he had done with the wounded, only the things that happened when he went on leave, always ending his stories with a wink and "Ooh la la!" Of course, if you told Alex that the sun rises in the east, he would say that he could prove that it didn't. He was a true contrarian, with reasoning that sounded so good it made you stop and think and wonder if he might possibly be right.

We were a typical family growing up in a middle class neighborhood. I attended P.S. 152, which was directly across the street from Midwood High School, later to be my alma mater, which is in turn directly across the street from Brooklyn College. We did what every good and obedient Jewish family did: we went to Temple three times a year, attended religious instruction, were Bar and Bat Mitzvah'd, and on Sundays we religiously went out for Chinese food.

Despite what some mean children had to say about her, my sister Lonni was not fat. She was what was called *zaftig*—a little overweight, but pleasingly so. We loved each other and always will. I loved all the attention her friends gave me when they were thirteen and I was eighteen. She was the baby and no one ever picked on her without suffering the wrath of her two older brothers, a situation that in later years proved a little intimidating for her dates. She was talented and happy and fun to be with. She had a calling for the stage from the time she was four. She laughed and sang and generally made you feel like you were the most important person in the world when you were with her.

Years later, when I was activated by the Red Cross on 9/11 and responded to Ground Zero as an EMT on day three, Lonni pleaded with me to get her credentials as a volunteer for the Red Cross so that she could help. I did. She spent over nine months working at whatever sites they assigned her to. Like so many who faced that tragedy and the uncertain days that followed, she disregarded her own safety and just did whatever was needed of her.

It was Lonni who acquired the Hungarian temper from my mom. She fought for everyone's rights, and was a successful advocate for New York policemen and firemen. She lobbied successfully for the Heart Act, making sure that those brave people who suffered heart attacks if not actually on the job at the time, but as a result of the job, would receive the benefits they deserved; was a social worker for New York City; had awful taste in men; and fought with anyone who crossed her. And, if you had four legs, she would adopt you.

3

But Seriously, Folks...My Career as a Stand-Up Comic

I HAD AN amazingly pedestrian life until one day when I was twelve, riding my bike to Hebrew School for my Bar Mitzvah lessons, I was hit by a car. I was in a coma for four days, which my brother swears actually knocked some sense into me. But my father became a different person with me after that. When we were alone, he was quiet and physically caring, gave lots of hugs and tickling, and from then on he never yelled at me even if I had done something wrong. It has taken me decades to understand (until I had my own children) why he always managed to make the most of the time we spent together after that. I survived the accident, and he and I realized just how much we loved each other. Sometimes it takes a major trauma to make you realize how incredibly deep your love for one another reaches.

I remember waking up in the hospital to see a crowd of people I did not recognize. They were also members of my school class coming to visit and bring me get-well cards they had made. My mother was there, and I said hi to everyone, and they all started yelling something about a miracle. A nurse hurried in and told them to settle down, saw that my eyes were open, and rushed out to get the doctor.

I don't remember much more about the hospital except that I could not wait to get home. I do remember the party they had for me that next week. All the relatives came. Arsenic came first and left early. Old Lace must have been waiting outside since she came in immediately after. Many of my classmates from school came and many neighbors came, folks who I later learned had taken turns bringing my mom to the hospital. Some neighbors I did not know, but there was plenty of food and drink and the party was great. People kept asking me if I'd seen a white light and questions like that, and I will tell it to you straight from the hip: I saw nothing. *Nada. Zip. Gornish.* I experienced the coma as nothing but a lot of blank time.

My mother swore that I'd survived because I was too stubborn to not have a big Bar Mitzvah party and get all those presents. She also told me that I had a guardian angel, her grandmother, who would always watch over me. The family called her Bubbie. I didn't find out for another decade that my great grandmother was a Hungarian gypsy, which I believe explains a lot about me.

In high school I was lucky enough to be placed in a new and unique educational program called the Experience Curriculum. Instead of merely reading about government, we actually went to Albany to watch our politicians in action. We went to City Hall in New York City. We went to Washington, DC, to see the White House and Congress and the Supreme Court. It was new and exciting. What's more, we learned to think independently, an experience I like to believe is responsible for the reasoning and logic behind some of my decisions. The program was admittedly a little bit unconventional and we would sometimes run into trouble on standardized tests. I loved the challenges but it did put many of us outside the mainstream of the rest of the students at the high school. After freshman year, we joined the rest of the classes in the "normal" curriculum, which I found boring by comparison. I played a lot of sports, barely started dating, and have no memory of anything sufficiently life-changing so as to mold my character. *That*, I was soon to find out, was waiting just around the corner.

At seventeen, I was an incredibly shy kid. Painfully so, according to my brother, who insisted, in an attempt to get me out of my shell, that I take part in my high school variety show. Over many, many protestations on my part he prevailed, and he spent months coaching me to do a short comedy act. I practiced telling a few jokes and did a pantomime to Danny Kaye and Spike Jones records. The big day arrived, and I must have been good, because the audience applauded quite enthusiastically! They brought me back for an encore for which I hadn't really prepared, so I ad-libbed and they applauded a lot more. I was standing with my mom, dad, brother, and sister after the show, and they were telling me how good I had been and asking why I had been hiding all this talent, when a very attractive woman came over and said she was a talent scout—she told me how natural I appeared on stage and how funny I was, and asked if I would be interested in trying out for a USO troupe. With shock and awe, my father quickly said, "May I have your business card? We will call you." We got into the car and the first words my dad said were, "Over my dead body are you going to go into show business!" But before anyone could say anything else, my mother said, "Irving, let's wait until we get home to discuss this."

When we got home, my parents went into the sun parlor, where all the family's life-changing conversations took place, and my brother and sister and I went into the kitchen. After what seemed like an eternity, my mother came into the kitchen and shooed my siblings out of the room. She looked at me with the most serious grin and said, "All your father wants is that you will promise him that you will go to college." I agreed, tried out, and was hired as a stand-up comic! I entertained with the troupe as often as I could for the next five years while simultaneously enlisting in the army and then attending college. I worked at all the military bases in the area, as well as children's hospitals and veterans' hospitals, and since the USO did not pay for our services, they acted as my talent agent and would get me gigs at many long-forgotten local nightclubs and midnight shows in the Borscht Belt at one of the lesser hotels. I remember I did a lot of dialect jokes. I could do very good Jewish and Italian accents, and double-talk in Swedish and German.

The worst audience I ever worked was a Hadassah women's luncheon. I was working all my straight stuff and they were looking at me, daring me to make them laugh. I hated doing it, but I tried an off-color joke and they instantly applauded. A real comedian hates stooping to dirty jokes, but sometimes it's the only way to go. The *best* audience was at a nightclub called the China Lantern in Brooklyn, New York. It was a birthday party for some important Italian person. The place held between two hundred and three hundred people. I started with a few Italian jokes in dialect and had the audience going until I switched to Jewish humor. The woman at the head table was laughing so hard I had to quip, "I love how hard she is laughing. I only hope her underwear is waterproof." This caused even more chaos. Her husband was stone-faced and I worried that I'd picked on the wrong person, so I tried to break the tension by asking, "Do you know how to make an Italian yo-yo? Tie a meatball to a strand of spaghetti." I destroyed the place. Only after the show I learned that the guest of honor—whom I had insulted—was a member of the local Mafia family. As I was leaving from backstage after the show, the, um, *gentleman* came back, suggested that I must have a large set of *cojones,* told me how funny he thought I was, and handed me a twenty.

I never did make a living in show business, but I met some incredible people, loved every minute of it, and began a lifelong love of the stage in its many forms. I conducted charitable goods and services auctions for over twenty years for churches, temples, schools, fire and ambulance corps, and sports figures' personal charities. I have provided comic relief in local theater productions. I lectured for the Office of Court Administration annual judges training school, for the Palm Beach County Bar Association, and for Palm Beach Community College's Lifelong Learning Program, as well as at Florida Atlantic University, at the Palm Beach County Speakers Bureau, at many private country clubs, and the Delray Beach Public Library, just to name a few. Presently I am a freelance lecturer. I used to say, "Have mike; will hike!" Now that I am older my slogan is, "Have gavel; will travel."

College is mostly a blur for me. I went to NYU in Washington Square and I guess I was rather a hippie. Now, that does not mean that I was stoned *all* the time, though I was known to attend my fair share of parties—this may account for why I do not remember much. I really worked hard at college. My brother had suggested that I do not take prelaw courses as much as psychology courses, since they would do me more good when dealing with clients than something like "Accounting for Lawyers."

In college, I learned to love folk music and cappuccino, quiet walks in Washington Square Park, *great* parties, and the Clancy Brothers and Tommy Makem. One evening I had invited Dik to join me to hear them, and after the show we hung around, and somehow or other Dik had volunteered to drive all the Clancy Brothers and Tommy Makem—all of 'em—to their hotel in Midtown Manhattan. Dik had a convertible at the time and some of us may have had a bit too much to drink, and so we all piled in on top of one another, and the Clancy Brothers and Tommy Makem decided to pay for the ride by singing. Unforgettable!

We were not stopped by the police, but can you imagine if a New York City Irish cop had stopped us and asked, "Now lads, what do ya think you all be doin'?" We would either have been arrested for the booze or the passenger count—or he would have joined us in a song or two and would then send us on our way.

I worked for Goldman Sachs on Wall Street for a short time and hated it. After that I worked for William A. White and Sons on 42nd Street, in real estate, specifically commercial leasing. While I made good money for a while, ultimately I found it boring.

It was about a year later that I decided to keep my promise to my dad about returning to law school. Classes were held at night for four years, a time in which I insisted on paying most of my own tuition and I had sometimes two or three part-time jobs during the day—process server, claims adjuster, and law clerk. I am not complaining. We all were having a rough time going to class at night. I have made some lifelong friends from those classes, probably because of the mutual hardships we complained about, but more likely for the help and support we gave each other.

Fordham Law School provides their students with a complete background of study and they make sure that graduates are ready to go out in the world and succeed. They are tough and tougher. The Jesuit influence was present—our course on ethics was tinged strongly with Catholicism. I graduated with the best education in the law that I can imagine, and *that* shaped my legal thinking almost as much as my dad did. I am very proud of my alma mater.

I go to my class reunions and always am amazed at how old my classmates look. I personally have not changed. They have.

4

Riding Homicide: Twenty-Four Hours of Hands-On Horror

After I graduated law school, I started working as a criminal law investigator for the Brooklyn district attorney's office. Three years in the district attorney's office taught me everything I'd ever wanted to know about the criminal justice system.

A law school graduate becomes a criminal law investigator while waiting to pass the New York State bar exam, and I existed in this limbo—not really a lawyer, not really a DA (as it turned out, an *unarmed* non-DA)—but something in between. The man who taught you the something in between was Ed Panzarella.

Ed was the bureau chief in charge of the recruits. No one liked Ed, and Ed felt pretty much the same way about them. Now, a person does not get a job in the Brooklyn DA's office because of law school grades, native intelligence, or even good looks. You got the job through a process known as *political placement.* At that time, you applied through the Democratic leader of Kings County, Meade Esposito. My dad had not been active in political circles but my godfather, Colonel Leon Freedman, had. Meade was the boss of the Democratic Party in Brooklyn and wielded enormous influence. The colonel got me the interview with Meade and I got the job. The colonel seemed to have all the right connections in Democratic politics.

The first thing you had to do as a criminal law investigator (a "CLI") was paperwork. It was boring and repetitive, and after three months you begged to be allowed to see a courtroom, even if only to watch an arraignment or a misdemeanor trial. Ed would just look at the papers on his desk and growl, "I'll tell you when you are ready not to embarrass me!"

For some reason, Ed must have had a soft spot in his heart for me because he sent me out in my fourth month on what he called *riding homicide* or what *we* called *twenty-four hours of hands-on horror*. When a call came in about any violent crime or major felony, you and a stenographer went to the actual scene of the crime. Sometimes the victim or the dead body would still be there and sometimes you went to the hospital to speak to the victim. We learned to take witness statements, interview the police in charge of cases, talk to victims' families, and then discuss the case the next morning with Ed, who managed to stay on top of everything the CLIs did. When you rode homicide, you might respond to the scene of any major felony, such as a rape, murder, or bank robbery.

Most of the time, statements came from victims and witnesses. However, every so often there would be a defendant who wanted to talk to a DA, not the police. At those times a green CLI's stomach gets tied up in knots for fear of making a mistake. CLIs on duty after hours would get a call from the precinct where the crime occurred, and a DA's car would then pick them up at their homes for a ride to the scene or the station house. During the day, you used your own car. The driver was not a cop and neither he, nor I with my ballpoint pen, nor the stenographer with his machine was what we would consider *armed.* We would drive into the very heart of some of the worst parts of Brooklyn, and being on duty twenty-four hours meant that it could be 4:00 a.m. and we'd be going into Bedford-Stuyvesant or Red Hook or Brownsville. In those neighborhoods, if a driver could not pull up to the precinct steps, we would not get out of the car.

One night on duty, around 9:00 p.m., I got the call from a precinct in the Bushwick section of Brooklyn, which the cop who called labeled "possible suspicious homicide." (I never really understood that label. Is the victim possibly dead, or merely suspiciously dead?) Either way, I called the driver, and fifteen minutes later we were in transition not to the scene, but to the captain's office in the precinct, because the witnesses were there and besides, the body had already been moved.

Apparently, a sixteen-year-old named Eddie G. had died from a bullet wound in his head. There were three eyewitnesses, Fat Louie, Speedy, and Jersey Jake. This is not a Damon Runyon tribute—these are truly the names they gave me when we were first introduced, and getting their real names turned out to be a little bit of a chore. Each witness told an identical story: Eddie G. walked up to the three of them, who were sitting on a stoop at the time, and asked if they wanted to see a gun. They all said yes and he took his father's .45-caliber automatic from his waistband. They all looked at it, and then Eddie said, "Let's play Russian roulette!"

"Eddie, you cannot play Russian roulette with an automatic since there is always a bullet in the chamber. You need a revolver so that you can spin the cylinder," Fat Louie had said to Eddie.

"But this is the only gun I have," Eddie reportedly said. He put the gun to his temple and pulled the trigger, and I guess that's why they called him Crazy Eddie. We subsequently learned that Eddie had a long history of mental illness, had recently been released from a juvenile facility, and was supposed to be undergoing psychiatric treatment.

After I'd been there for about one year, Ed Panzarella called me to his office where I was the first to learn of his decision to retire. I was a Kings County (Brooklyn) Supreme Court trial assistant at that time, and he said I was the only one he had called. We talked for a long time about life and about cases he had had, and then he gave me the glass paperweight with the scales of justice embedded inside it that was on his desk. I still have it.

Finally, I cannot finish this chapter without telling you how I got buzzed on marijuana when I was in the Brooklyn DA's office.

Ed had assigned me to work with him and a large task force on a marijuana bust. The postal authorities had learned that a large package of marijuana was being shipped from California to New York. The FBI, Treasury agents, and cops from Brooklyn and Queens were all waiting at the airport to follow the package to the addressee. After the postal truck delivered the package, there were at least eight cops there hiding in the bushes when the "postman" identified himself as a cop and arrested the guy who signed for the package. Everyone then returned to Ed's office in Brooklyn. Understand, there were twelve of us in the room, all writing out reports. We were there for hours. So was ninety-six pounds of marijuana, in bricks, unwrapped, and sitting in the middle of the desk. When we finally left the building for a late meal, we were all buzzed. Just breathing in the fumes in that room did us all in.

After being a "grunt," I passed the bar exam and was assigned to the lower court bureau, a most intense and eye-opening experience. Again, as a newbie in the bureau you are assigned to night court. You arrive at 5:00 p.m. to review the night's caseload and at 6:00, you begin the incredible task of handling over 125 arraignments, bail settings, making recommendations to the judge, and arguing with the legal aid attorney. Every kind of case imaginable. I had a mother approach the railing separating the spectators from the attorneys and plead with me to keep her daughter in jail, since she was an addict and the mother hoped she could stay clean for a few days, since she was not going to bail her out. I had lawyers approach, wanting to plead their client guilty right away so that they would not have to spend time in jail and could be bailed out. There were always people crying in court, angry faces, victims with bandages, and very bored looking policemen—bored since they had just finished mountains of paperwork and wanted to go home. It was also the most diverse learning experience. Over the course of a few months, I learned more about people there than in the sociology courses I had taken in college. I learned how to be more patient than I had ever been and learned to do three things at once, since in three hours and across 125 cases, you were a) reading the next file while you were b) telling the judge what you thought bail should be set at in the present case, and c) writing up the notes from the last case. This might sound a little perverse, but I enjoyed the challenge and think I may have become a better lawyer for it.

I graduated from the lower court bureau and was assigned to the grand jury bureau. I will skip that job description for the time being, since there is a lot to discuss about grand juries later in the book.

I then graduated to the Kings County, Brooklyn, Supreme Court trial bureau. This was a major advancement and unusual for someone to move so rapidly through those steps in the office. I was very proud, and so were my father and brother.

One of the earliest cases assigned to me was a real can of worms. What else did I expect as a (you guessed it) *newbie* in the bureau? I hope by this time that you have learned that everyone in a district attorney's office has to pay their dues when they are the new kid on the block, and I never again expected anything less. It turned out that the case I referred to became a springboard for my career, with front-page coverage in *El Diario* and congratulations from everyone from the bureau chief to Eugene Gold, the district attorney.

The infamous Juan Contreres had set up an office in a largely Spanish-speaking section of Brooklyn and made up phony credentials, purporting to be an attorney. His sign outside the storefront read *Abogado* and *La Inmigración* (immigration attorney). He was, in fact, a complete fraud. He had no credentials and no higher education of any sort—just a con man. In his several years of operating, he defrauded about 1,500 immigrants. He would promise to bring families to the United States and promise green cards to illegal aliens. He charged them whatever the traffic would bear—never too much or too little—but we estimated that he averaged over $150,000 for every one hundred people he bilked. The case was handed to me because of the difficulty in getting witnesses to testify against him and the fact that I spoke broken Spanish. Most of the illegal aliens had been deported and the majority of the people remaining here were too afraid of him to talk to us. I had a really great team of detectives who wanted to nail this criminal and who voluntarily put in a lot of overtime. We finally found about five victims who would testify, but only after we found the first one in a little village in Mexico. Because I promised to protect all the witnesses, I will not use their actual names. "Pablo" had voluntarily returned to his village in "Mexico" to be with his family since Contreres had failed for years to bring them to America as he had promised to do. My detective called the Alcalde of the village (the mayor) and asked for the phone number for Pablo. Since I was listening on the phone, I had to ask what the mayor was saying after he stopped laughing. My detective looked at me and told that there was only one phone in the entire village. The detective asked the mayor to get Pablo to come to the phone. The mayor said yes but he would have to go fetch him, explaining that his car was not working and he would have to go by bicycle. He also explained that although the call had gone through this time, the phone service was not very reliable and that we should stay on the line. We agreed and forty-five minutes later (think of the phone bill the DA's office got that month,) the mayor returned with Pablo. Pablo told us how he had gone to see the *abogado* to try to bring his family into the United States. He described Contreres's office as having what looked like many diplomas on the wall, identifying Contreres as an attorney specializing in immigration law. He stated that Contreres told him that he could bring Pablo's family to the US without any problems, and told him it would cost $1,000. Pablo got the money, returned, and paid it to Contreres.

He returned several months later to ask about the progress Contreres was making and Contreres told him it would cost another $750 to get all the proper papers. Pablo paid him again and waited. He and all the other clients waited. Contreres never delivered for any of them. He never filed a single document with immigration that brought any family members to the United States, nor did he obtain any green cards for any of them. With the consent of Pablo, the district attorney, my detectives, and the US government, we flew Pablo to Brooklyn and put him in a hotel with a lot of security. He was able to contact friends of his in the Spanish community and convince them that since he was going to testify against Contreres, they would be safe doing the same. I ended up with five people testifying, and after what seemed like a long trial, the jury convicted him and he was sent to state prison. The Spanish community was very happy that we had finally convicted this crook, who had not only stolen money from so many of them, but had given them false hopes and dreams. I received many congratulatory calls from that community and was declared *mas importante* to their people.

There is a huge amount of joy for a prosecutor who has brought justice to so many unfortunate victims. More importantly, that community learned that they could trust the authorities.

5

The Woman Behind the Man

In 1969, the second miraculous event of my life took place. The first, as you recall, was coming out of a coma when I was a kid. This time my miracle was to last over thirty years.

I had graduated from law school and was still single. Now, those who are not of the Jewish faith may not know this, but it is the holy obligation of every Jewish female to make sure that "eligible" Jewish males do not remain so. Therefore, I had more than my share of aunts and cousins and friends of the family setting me up on blind dates. I tried to say no to as many invitations as possible, but one time Uncle Moses Leavitt's wife, Fannie, was at a bar mitzvah on Long Island that my family attended, and my dad asked me if I would drive my aunt home to New York City. We had a pleasant and interesting conversation, and when we got to her apartment house on the Upper East Side she told me that there was a lovely young lady from a very fine family that she wanted me to meet. She was gently persuasive so I agreed to call, and after waiting a day or two, I did.

Her name was Edith Schur, but all her friends called her Taffy. Although we spoke on the phone for a very long time, I still was reluctant to commit to any blind date, but finally she agreed to let me pick her up at her apartment on Park Avenue for a short dinner date. To call where her family lived an *apartment* is misleading. I have lived in houses that were smaller than that apartment! It came with a maid and cook. I had been on so many "bad" blind dates that I thought that I might need an out. This was, of course, before cell phones, so I set it up so that not long after I arrived, my friend Tony would call their home phone with a concocted story—something about the DA's office having called and that I had to respond to a crime scene.

From the moment I looked into her powder-blue eyes, I started praying that Tony would forget to call me.

It wasn't that I fell into her blue eyes and was captured; she was lovely all over. She was so smart and so gentle, so talented and so giving. The maid escorted me into the living room, where I met Taffy, her mother, and her father. Ira Schur asked what my favorite drink was and I was so flustered that all I could think of was J&B Scotch. He apologized—he did not have any J&B, but would a twenty-five-year-old Chivas Regal suffice? Then her parents gave me the third degree, asking me about myself. At that moment the phone rang, and the maid arrived to announce that the call was for me, but I was busy falling in love and I certainly did not want to leave.

It was an urgent call. Yes, that would be Tony's way. I was left making my excuses and assured Taffy that I would call her if it was not too late that night.

I called her at around eleven and we talked on the phone until two.

I knew I was in love after the first few dates. So did she. All we had to do was work on our two families. Mine was a cinch—everyone loved her immediately. Her family was a slightly different story. Her mother Ethel remarked to her that she thought I was a boy from Brooklyn and that I was, in her opinion, "swarthy." To this day I do not really understand what she meant by that, but I know it could not have been good. Taffy's sister Jane, meanwhile, never had a kind word for me (and no one has anything particularly nice to say about her), but her sister Susan and I have become fast friends over the years. It took a while, but I think we love each other as dearly as if we were brother and sister.

Her father and I got along too, especially in his later years. He was a brilliant and very successful accountant and a published amateur photographer, with an unerring way of kindly cutting you down before you realized it. I would be visiting my in-laws and would bring a bunch of snapshots from a trip we took or a birthday party of one of my girls, and Ira would very patiently look at them and then pronounce, "Well, it is a record of the event." That said, he taught me an enormous amount about photography and it was his keen eye and critiques that have led to some of the photographs I'm most proud of today. As the years went by and I was successful in my law practice, I had earned respect from him. When we were able to spend some private time together, Ira taught me about the stock market and investing and he would ask me legal questions about stories that were in the news. It took a while, but we were able to build a relationship that I never had with Ethel. I think she wanted Taffy to marry a prince.

For our first two real dates, Taffy introduced me to *La Bohème* and I took her to night court in Brooklyn. She sang to me and I made her laugh with my Borscht Belt humor. We loved and we laughed. We traveled and we planned. I talked her ear off and she listened. I dreamed my dreams with her that night forty-two years ago, and she always helped to make them happen. She knew me and always told me that whatever my next goal was, I would attain it and she would help make it happen. She did. When they talk about *the woman behind the man*, they are talking about Taffy. I could not have been luckier to have found her. She gave me two beautiful daughters, Karen and Amy. She crafted, created, nursed, and nurtured our children and our marriage, and made everything work.

We talked about our childhoods and families; we planned our lives and our future. We were so careful to try never to go to bed angry if we had had an argument. (It was usually my fault.) We discussed politics and Broadway plays. We talked about everything. We communicated and promised not to ever hold anything back from each other. It worked. Taffy had a touch with people that is hard to find. The girls and I referred to her as IMFE—"I make friends everywhere." And she did, whether in an airport waiting room or at a restaurant, with the utmost sincerity and true interest in everyone she met.

I learned so many life lessons from this (much nicer than I) gentle soul. So if you want to know about the important influences that shaped my life, you also have to look at Taffy.

We grew together in Chappaqua, New York, with kids and collies, courts and community volunteerism—very good friends and a lively private practice of law in that small town.

I did give that lovely lady a bit of anxiety when I announced that I was going to become a volunteer fireman. I attended fire training for eight weeks and spent the next ten years in the department fighting brush fires, house fires, car fires, and would run out of my office in the middle of a real estate closing if the alarm went off. My associates would know to take over and I never had a client complain. As I mention elsewhere in this book, I was injured in a house fire and developed smoke sensitivity, so naturally I then joined the volunteer ambulance corps. One hundred and twenty-eight hours of school later, I was a certified Emergency Medical Technician. Taffy would awaken with me in the middle of the night when my pager went off and would always be there for me when I returned from the call, to talk to me and make sure I was okay. The words *understanding* and *sympathetic* do not come close to the caring nature she had.

I do know that she and the girls were happy to have me out of the fire department and thought it would be safer for me to be in the ambulance corps. They were right about safer, but not about the emotional energy one had to spend in that business. She was still always there and always encouraging about anything I wanted to accomplish. I think that way of her thinking helped me enormously in my job as a judge, and certainly helped me become the man I am today.

6

THE PROSECUTION OF FRANK SACCO

I HAD SOME wonderful and some awful experiences during the three years I spent as an assistant district attorney in Westchester County. When my wife and I decided to move to the "country" (still considered country, long before The Clintons moved to our small town and put it on the map), I applied for a job in the DA's office. I remember Chief Assistant District Attorney Tom Facelle interviewing me. He spent a lot of time asking how many major cases I had been exposed to and how many murder cases I had tried. I told him Brooklyn was averaging over three hundred homicides a year; he told me that Westchester was averaging eight a year. He asked how much time I usually got to prepare a case for trial, and I told him that the file would be handed to you on a Friday and you were then told to be ready to go to trial on Monday—if you were lucky. Sometimes I wouldn't see the material until the day before—and twice I got a file in the morning to start the hearings and trial in the afternoon!

Tom Facelle seemed to like everything I said and told me that while it was very unusual to tell an applicant that he was being hired on the spot, he *did* want me to meet the DA, Carl Vergari, and he told me that he was sure that I'd get the job. I met with Carl and have the utmost respect for both of them, not because they hired me (which was of course brilliant on their part), but because they are two men of honesty, integrity, and fair-mindedness in a world that needs more people in power like them.

I got the job and we found a house in Chappaqua—a three-bedroom fieldstone ranch that cost us $64,000, the best investment I have ever made! We didn't want to raise a family in the city, if we could help it, and Chappaqua turned out to be the perfect place to call home and raise our girls.

I was assigned to the trial bureau and immediately learned that my appointment had repercussions. First, I was an outsider to the other assistants and I was from *Brooklyn.* Second, there were other junior assistants that had been waiting for the slot I was given, and third, I was the only Jewish assistant in the bureau. Now I am not saying that *all* the other assistants held these factors against me, only the ones who woke up in the morning and came to work. It took a full six months and several trials for me to begin to win some grudging respect.

Eventually some of them welcomed me into their ranks—well, most of them, anyway—and I made some very good friends there. I mention these sour grapes only to help explain a case that was assigned to me for trial.

One day I was summoned to the office of Anthony Molea, the trial part bureau chief. He asked me if I had tried any cases against organized crime in the three years that I was in the Brooklyn DA's office. I laughed out loud and asked him if he was serious. (As I later learned, Anthony was not the kind of bureau chief you asked, "Are you serious?") After I stopped laughing I told him that I had been involved many times in trying organized crime cases and that it was something I thought I could do.

Anthony then proceeded to tell me about the Frank Sacco investigation. Frank was an alleged member of organized crime; he was suspected of being a member of the Genovese crime family, and the authorities suspected that he had murdered Robert Meloni, believed to be an associate of Frank's. He had not been charged with that crime, but an assistant DA in the office had been part of a yearlong investigation into Frank's loan sharking activities. Anthony asked me to go to Assistant District Attorney (ADA) Lou Cherico's office to be briefed and to see if we could try the case together. Cherico was in the Rackets Bureau therefore had his own small office.

I walked into Cherico's office and the first thing I noticed, after looking at this obviously ex-marine type, was the hand grenade on his desk. No, not a pencil cup or a stapler, but a really scary looking, very authentic-looking hand grenade, a World War Two–type of "pineapple", and on it was inscribed, "Take a number." On the pin a tag said "One." With this totem on his desk, he made it clear just how your interruption was going to make him feel.

Cherico was not happy with the situation. He wanted to try the case himself but Molea lacked confidence in his abilities as a trial attorney. He grudgingly told me about the many months of wiretaps and the dozens of interviews he had conducted. He said that he didn't think I could become familiar enough with the case in time to try it since the trial date was only five weeks away. This time I did not laugh out loud.

We went back to Molea's office. Lou told Molea that he wanted to try the case himself and did not need me. Anthony waited and eventually asked me what I thought. When I replied that I thought it was a very complicated case and that I would not mind having Lou as second chair, I thought Lou was going to kill me with a look. Anthony asked me to wait outside his office and a few minutes later Lou emerged red in the face and told me it was my turn to go in and see the boss.

Our conversation was very short. Lou and I would be trying the case together and I'd need to work out the details. I walked into Cherico's office and in my best Brooklyn-commanding tone said, "I'll pick the jury and we can split up the witnesses!" He agreed, but I think no one had dared speak to him like that since his military days. I was relieved that grenade on his desk turned out not to be real!

I, meanwhile, thought I was in prosecutors' heaven, with five whole weeks to prepare for trial. What luxury! I read the tapes and the statements in the first week and interviewed the witnesses for the next three weeks and discovered the weakness within the case. There is always a weakness within a case, and this was it: The witnesses were either scared or hostile. Not one of them wanted to testify against Frank Sacco. It took cajoling, threats, and sheer intimidation to get them to talk to me. I had them promise me that they would at least repeat their grand jury testimonies at trial.

I picked a jury, and after every session Lou would tell me how much he disagreed with my selections of jurors. He would then storm out of the empty courtroom to go report to Molea, but, having grown a thick skin in Brooklyn, I brushed it off, trusting my instincts.

At the time, Frank Sacco was in federal custody on unrelated charges so his guards were federal marshals. They were overheard by the court officers telling Frank that the rules were simple: once they took the handcuffs off in the courthouse, if Frank wandered more than six feet away from wherever they were, they would put a bullet in the back of his head.

Picture the courtroom. It's the usual setup, but at Frank's defense table stands Frank in his $900 sharkskin suit (today, the equivalent of a $2000 suit). His attorney, Vincent Lanna, and the two marshals standing behind him are also wearing suits. The jury realizes that no court officers are close at hand, and they get an impression of a less-than-dangerous defendant. At the prosecutor's table, I stand beside a taller, skinny, redheaded guy, Lou Cherico, an obvious military type, surrounded on the table and the floor by piles of files and boxes of papers.

In his opening statement, Lanna tells the jury that Frank was merely helping people out who could not get a loan from a bank. I, in turn, tell them that Frank is a loan shark. They look confused already.

For over a week and a half Lou and I alternate putting witnesses on the stand, including a great many forensic and wiretap specialists, and I put the first four victims on the stand. Each one of them testifies. Yes, they had gotten loans from Frank but only after they had tried for bank loans, family loans, insurance company loans, and so forth. They make Frank sound like the neighborhood choirboy helping these poor people out of a jam. Well yes, they admitted, it was true that he charged a lot of interest. Yes, it was true they had been persuaded to sign over their property and cars when they couldn't pay the interest to Frank.

The jury is giving me looks as if to ask, "Why are you picking on this nice man?"

On the day before the appearance of my last witness, "Robert" (the victim who we felt had lost the most to Frank), I received a call from a detective who told me the witness wanted to see me before he testified, and could the detective bring him to my office? I told him yes and began to worry that we were about to lose the case. I had no idea what I was about to learn.

Robert arrived and sat down with Lou and me in my office and we learned why he was so determined to speak with us. We sent him home with instructions to the detective to deliver him to court the next morning.

The following morning, Robert took the stand, and when I looked around I noticed that the courtroom was filled. Anthony Molea himself was there and almost every reporter who had covered the story had shown up. I began questioning Robert, and Vinnie Lanna, the defense attorney, immediately began objecting to almost every question I asked. I managed to go through all the preliminaries about Robert trying to keep his restaurant alive and borrowing from the bank, from family, and from friends, then selling whatever he could, and finally in desperation going to Frank for a loan. When he couldn't pay the weekly interest—*vig* as it's known—Frank would go to Robert's house and start taking things. Frank had him sign over the titles to his car and his wife's car, had him empty the children's college savings, and took his wife's jewelry. Frank was eventually arrested but was released on bail prior to his being arrested by the feds. The investigation revealed that Robert was one of Frank's victims, and the DA decided to call Robert to testify. Robert had told the DA that he was reluctant to testify and was willing only to repeat to the jury what he had said in the grand jury.

By now I felt as if my jury hated me for picking on the local lender who, even though he was a rough businessman, "just tried to help people out." I walked up to the witness box and quietly asked Robert if he had seen or spoken to Frank after his initial arrest. Vinnie Lanna almost jumped out of his seat with objections. Following a long sidebar conference, Judge Evans Brewster overruled the objections. So, Robert went on to testify that before Frank had been taken into federal custody, Frank had called him and demanded a meeting. Robert was afraid to go, but too afraid of Frank not to. Robert testified that Frank stared him straight in the face and said, "If you testify against me, I will have you killed!"

You could actually feel the change in the jury at that moment. I knew that they now understood who and what Frank was. Robert went on to say that he was reluctant to testify but that when Frank threatened his life, that was the last straw. He had already lost everything, his business, his life savings, his kids' college savings, and he felt he had to tell the world what had happened.

Given the evidence and Robert's testimony that the jury had heard, I probably did not have to deliver a closing argument, but I did.

The jury found him guilty of five counts of making usurious loans. Each count carried with it a separate sentence of four years in state prison. All the reporters rushed out of the courtroom when the guilty verdict was announced. Lou grudgingly shook my hand. Anthony Molea walked over to counsel table as I was gathering our files and congratulated me.

The next set of events still mystifies me.

The courtroom cleared out. Lou took some of the files and left me with the rest of them. I wanted to let Taffy know that I had convicted Frank so I walked into the back room of the court where the clerk's office was to use the telephone. Just as Taffy got on the phone and I managed to get out the words, "I won the case," Frank walked into the office with his two marshals. He had heard me and asked, "That your wife?"

I answered him that it was.

Frank reached his hand out, the marshals watching him every second. Because Frank was an intimidating character, when he reached out for something you generally gave him whatever was in your hand.

I handed him the phone.

He took it, and as God is my witness, the following conversation took place.

"Hello Mrs. Leavitt? This is Frank Sacco. Your husband won a big victory today. (Pause.) Yeah, I am not mad at him—he just did his job without being vicious. By the way, *mah-nish-tah-naw ha-laila ha-zeh*!"

Why is this night different from all other nights?

"Yeah, I know about your Passover holiday. Well—goodbye." He handed the phone back to me, and Taffy asked me, "Was that really Frank Sacco?" I do not think she ever got over that call.

On sentencing day, Judge Brewster sentenced Frank to four years on each count of usury, to be served consecutively, a total of twenty years for ruining the lives of so many families.

Several months later, I was at home when Taffy answered the phone and called into the living room that an FBI agent wished to speak to me. I got on the phone and the agent told me not to worry, but Frank Sacco had escaped from jail. Even though they had found a list Frank had made of one hundred people he was mad at, I wasn't on it. I wonder to this day if Lou Cherico was on that list. Later that year Frank was recaptured.

7

The Wisdom of a Lower Court Judge

But enough about me for now. Let's talk about you and your perceptions. I have learned that the media, Hollywood, television, and many mystery writers have given you an absolutely slanted view of our justice system. I hope in the next few chapters to give you some basic knowledge of our system and perhaps share a few trade secrets from the other side of the bench. Perhaps after the next few chapters, you'll decide that if you want an evening's entertainment, you'll forget the movies or TV and attend night court instead, which is always open to the public.

I was nominated and campaigned for Town Judge in the town of New Castle, a hamlet of Chappaqua, NY. It was an election like any other in a small town. One has to go to Lions Club and Rotary meetings, all the places of worship in town, large cookouts, fundraising cocktail parties for the candidates and finally you have to knock on a lot of doors and hand out your literature and campaign gimmick if you had one (which, it might not surprise you, I did – pencils with a dual-tipped eraser on the end, shaped like a gavel!). I was fortunate enough to win and started my judicial career in New Castle, New York, the fulfillment of a lifelong dream to become a judge.

Town Court, also known as the people's court, can be called village court, traffic court, or local court as well. It is the only court that most people will ever participate in. Town Courts generally handle traffic cases, small claims actions, code violations, misdemeanor cases, preliminary felony cases, and bail settings. Town judges issue search warrants, sometimes at 2:30 a.m. In my jurisdiction, the judges were on call constantly but actual court time was once a week if you didn't have a trial scheduled.

As a Town Judge, I needed to have a court clerk who could handle a million details and questions, deal with the attorneys (who always wanted to have their cases called first), talk with the police officers (who were on overtime), and on and on. These courts handle all these cases and huge amounts of paperwork, sometimes with very little clerical help other than the court clerk. Clerks do a remarkable job and have to have a huge amount of patience. Clerks listen to sad stories and remarkable excuses for defendants' misdeeds. Some of the justifications stretch credibility, but others make you take a step back and realize how hard life has become for some people.

There are moments when judges can really enjoy their time in court. The funniest moment I have ever had gave us something to laugh about whenever we met someone new to tell the story to, and it was one of my dad's favorite stories from my time on the bench. New Castle had enacted a new law that stated that all homeowners had to keep their dog either under voice and visual control or on a leash at all times. Some months after it was enacted, I entered the courtroom for what I thought was a normal session. There were about a hundred people present, including a reporter from the *Chappaqua Journal* in the front row, hoping for a story to print. Next to him was my dad, who always liked coming to watch me preside. I looked out and saw a man in the back of the courtroom with a dog on a leash. Not a Seeing Eye dog or a companion dog, just a dog on a leash in my courtroom! I whispered to my court clerk Evelyn, "Who is that?" She informed me that it was the first case being tried under the new leash law. The crowd had not seen the dog yet, so for the moment I still had control of the courtroom.

I told her to call that case first so as to get the dog out of the courthouse. She called the case, and as the man and his dog approached, there was a small tittering in the room and the *Chappaqua Journal* reporter had found his story. I stated, "Mr. Smith, you are charged with a violation of town law, failure to keep your dog under voice and visual control or to have him on a leash. How do you plead?"

"Not guilty, Your Honor!" the man replied.

"Very well sir, I will set this case down for trial," I said.

"What does that mean?" he asked. By this time, the crowd was openly laughing and the reporter was writing down every word.

"That means that the dog warden who arrested your dog is not here tonight and she is the witness in this case."

"That means I have to come back again?" he whined. "I had to leave work early to get here! This is not fair." The dog stood there, looking mildly interested.

I was now losing control of the courtroom. I would have done almost anything to get him out! Everyone was laughing, even the reporter. I looked at the defendant and said, "I'll tell you what. Show me that your dog obeys you and I will dismiss the ticket."

"That's fair," he said, and looked at the dog. "Sit, Benjamin!"

Nothing. The dog was not moving.

"Sit, boy, sit. Sit!" His voice rising...... Nothing.

The courtroom got completely out of control. The reporter was writing furiously.

I looked at the dog owner and gently said, “It does not look as if your dog obeys your voice commands.”

He looked at me with a straight face and said, “I forgot to tell you, Judge: the dog is deaf!”

That’s lower court, folks. Yes, I dismissed the case. In the interest of “justice.”

After he retired, my dad would come to Chappaqua, have dinner with us, and then come to court with me. It was great having Dad in the courtroom, but I had to stop asking my mother to come to court. She wanted me to find everyone who had any plausible excuse for speeding *not guilty*. She would sit in the first row of the courtroom and send me not-so-subtle hand signals to be lenient. Mom was a person who did not want anyone to suffer or be unhappy. She told me that if I gave them a stern speech and let them go that they would probably not speed again. She said this with a wink and a grin.

Speaking of speeding tickets, I always think that I have heard more unique excuses for speeding than most judges—until I hear something new from another judge – who relates the excuses drivers have given to police – and realize that the mind of man is either incredibly stupid or extremely devious:

- “I have a sick child at home.”
- “I have a sick wife.”
- “I have a very sick husband.”
- “My dog is dying.”
- “My plants are dying.”
- “I have diarrhea.”
- “I am late for work.”
- “I am late coming *from* work.”
- “I am late to pick up my children.”
- And on and on, ad nauseam.

I remember one novel excuse from a defendant with an identical twin brother, who was accused of running into someone’s car and leaving the scene of the accident, only to be stopped five minutes later and telling the police officer, "I didn't do it! It must have been someone who looked just like me!"

I have been asked many times over the years to tell people the very best defense when being pulled over for speeding. Here it is! Plead not guilty, and on the day set for your trial, bring three friends to court with you, all dressed in suits. Get there early, find the officer who gave you the ticket, meet him before the trial, and greet him warmly. Tell him that the three people with you are expert witnesses in radar technology, nomographic charts, and velocities, and mention that after they testify, you are planning to ask for an adjournment to bring in two more expert witnesses.

Either that, or that you will be glad to plead guilty to a seat belt violation. Works every time.

After all the cases I've heard in traffic court and all the cases I've had to rule on, I cannot match the shortest decision ever handed down by a judge. This story was told to me by my very dear friend, Judge Dennis Donovan. The defendant made his final appeal to the court, "As God is my judge, I am not guilty!" The judge replied, "He isn't; I am; you are!"

Let's return to the serious side of lower courts.

DUI—driving under the influence, previously referred to as driving while intoxicated (DWI) —represents one of the most serious offenses in lower court. Did you know that the major cause of death of teenagers in this country is not blood disease, cancer, or heart attacks, but drunk driving? When you listen to the news and hear that a defendant just made bail after being arrested for his fifth DUI case and the accident involved physical injuries, you have to wonder if the judge should have worn a helmet during his high school football practices.

I may have strayed from the straight-and-narrow interpretation of the DUI statutes from time to time while staying within the law. Let's call it stretching not breaking. I, like many judges I've known, was especially incensed by the carnage caused by drunk drivers. At the sentencing of one drunk driving defendant, I ordered that he have a license plate frame made that said "CONVICTED DRUNK DRIVER." If I saw a car in front of me weaving across lanes of traffic with that plate, I sure as heck would know what the problem was. I thought my innovative sentence might discourage some people from driving drunk, and I received a lot of praise for this action. I thought that it was such a good idea, in fact, that I made it a condition of his probation. The defendant appealed and the court of appeals decided that I had exceeded my authority, calling it cruel and unusual punishment. Really? I never stopped trying innovative ideas. I discovered that it was the political world with all its power and money that I had to fight.

For many years, DUI was considered a social crime and treated very lightly by the courts. Since the inception of MADD and SADD (Mothers Against Drunk Driving and Students Against Destructive Decisions), that has changed, but not as much as it has in other countries. Try to imagine what it would be like in the United States if our punishments for drunk driving were like some that have at one time existed in the following countries:

In Australia, intoxicated drivers' names are printed in the local paper under the headline "He's Drunk and in Jail!" In Turkey, drunk drivers are taken twenty miles out of town and forced to walk back under police escort. Norwegian drunk drivers spend three weeks in jail at hard labor and lose their driver's licenses for one year. In Malaysia, the driver is jailed, and if he is married, his wife is jailed, too. In Russia, the drunk driver's license is revoked for life. In England, the sentence is one-year suspension of license, a $250 fine, and jail for one year. In Poland, the driver is fined, goes to jail, and is forced to attend political lectures. But at the top of the list is United Arab Emirates, likely because the government prohibits even the consumption of alcohol. As a result, a DUI charge can involve fines, long-term imprisonment and public flogging.

I tell the judges I lecture to that it should be mandatory for them to visit an emergency room on a Saturday night for a couple of hours and see the carnage drunk drivers cause, so that they will then sit in court with a new perspective. My most surprising drunk driving arraignment occurred when I was a volunteer with the Chappaqua ambulance corps and we pulled a drunk gentleman from his wrecked car. We took him to the hospital and the police handcuffed him to the stretcher. He was lucky—treated for minor injuries and released to the police. I was the judge who arraigned him the next day. I asked his lawyer if he wanted me to remove myself from the case since I had firsthand knowledge of the offense. The lawyer shocked me when he said no, stating, "He was your patient, so I think you will have sympathy for him." I stayed on the case.

Many of the criminal cases heard in lower court involve drugs—mostly marijuana, since it is a lesser offense. The laws against marijuana represent, in my opinion, an outrageous attempt by our government to stop us from harming ourselves. In 2013, in Florida alone, the police arrested 50,000 people for marijuana possession. From the time of our Puritan fathers, this nation has tried to control our "sins." Has outlawing prostitution been successful? No—we still have prostitution. How about when they made gambling illegal because of fears that the working class would lose all their money and not pay their rent or feed their children? Well, no, we still have gambling. How about Prohibition? Missed again! Prohibition helped create powerful organized crime in this country. Who are we kidding? When will we stop trying to legislate moral behavior?

This is not a running diatribe for the legalization of all drugs. It is simply a plea for common sense, for the realization that what we are doing doesn't work. I say if you can't beat 'em, join 'em. Take the profit out of illegal drugs, control them, and regulate them. I know of no legislator who is against medical marijuana who has had a family member, his or her spouse, or a child plead for relief from pain when they are going through chemotherapy and cannot keep food down. It's easy to be high and mighty from a pedestal. I cannot tell you what I would have done as a sitting judge if a member of my family had pleaded with me for medical marijuana, which was illegal in New York at that time, to help stop their suffering.

Finally, let's discuss trials in lower court. The vast majority of cases are heard by the judge alone. You can request a jury trial, and, in lower court, this is a jury of six people. Though rare, it does happen that someone might not trust the wisdom of a lower court judge (I say that tongue in cheek) and request a jury trial.

Judges in all courts, but mostly in lower courts, are asked to sign search warrants, usually at ungodly hours, and have these very hard decisions to make on the spot. I attended the National Judicial College for some graduate work and met judges from all over the country, including Texas. In one session, we began discussing search and seizure, the difficulty in obtaining a valid search warrant, and the pressure on judges to issue search warrants quickly (we've all seen *Law and Order*). At the lunch break during the session, a Texas judge described a Texas search warrant. In Texas, he said, the sheriff sends his deputy to the back door of the suspect's house, he bangs on the front door shouting, "Sheriff!" and his deputy shouts, "Y'all come on in!"

Since the lower courts deal with such a variety of cases and people, it would be remiss of me to belittle the incredible work that lower court judges do. They work hard and have long hours and little help on a relatively low salary. I applaud them. After all, I was one of them.

There are, however, some problems when you have to keep records of all the fines, penalties, and poundage that the court collects for the state and for victim restitution. This record keeping is the responsibility of the judge. I was attending a summer judge's training school when one of the lecturers from New York State's Division of audit and control described how hard it was for him to conduct field audits. He described one judge from a small town in Upstate New York who hadn't sent the correct amount of fines to the state. As the auditor was going through the books, he observed the letters *E.S.P.* on many of the pages. Confused, he asked the judge what extrasensory perception had to do with his accounting, and the judge replied, "No, no, that means Error Some Place!"

Let's talk about the grassroots-level of justice, the real "local court." Local court handles traffic offenses; violation of a city, town, or municipal ordinance; less serious criminal cases such as shoplifting; civil cases involving less than $15,000 (although each state is different); landlord-tenant disputes; and much more. There is a division of County Court called the Small Claims Division, in which people can bring their own lawsuits without an attorney, provided the dispute is less than $3,000.

A typical calendar in local court usually follows a format. The order is generally criminal cases first, then traffic violations, then civil matters. A stenographer is present to record all that is said and, when necessary, an interpreter will translate for a non-English speaking defendant or witness. In some of the smaller counties where there are budgetary constraints, having a live stenographer or an interpreter is sometimes not possible. One way to solve this is with a tape recorder.

Another way is a deal, as in "Have I got a deal for you!" When I sat as a local Town Judge in New Castle, New York, near the end of the fiscal year we had very little in the budget for an interpreter. When court convened, I would look out at the crowd and see seventy-five to one hundred people waiting for their cases to be called, most for traffic tickets. There was a small percentage of Hispanic people, and I would ask if anyone spoke both English and Spanish. Veterans of my courtroom (other than the current defendant) who knew what was coming, would immediately raise their hands. I would choose one and ask what kind of ticket he or she was appearing for. If it was a minor speeding ticket, I would happily announce that if they stayed to interpret, I would consider their acting as interpreter for the court as community service which would be strongly considered in their speeding ticket case. In other words: "Have I got a deal for you!" This was an eminently practical if not politically correct solution.

There are rewards to being a judge in lower court. You get to do a lot of weddings. Sometimes you even get asked to stay for the cocktail party. For those of you who have never campaigned for public office, who have not had the opportunity to attend a lot of formal dinners or all those rubber-chicken events, here's a tip from an insider: fill up on the hors d'oeuvres—they're the best part of the meal.

8

My Election: Let's Get On with It and Open the Bubbly!

The story of how I became a superior court judge is actually a very funny story, if a bit upsetting. I was elected twice to serve as the Town Judge of Chappaqua because of my great knowledge of the law (what I learned in Brooklyn), my immense good looks (I jest), and as I mentioned earlier, my unique campaign giveaway (the pencils with two "gavel" erasers at the end. My daughter tells me she still uses them (I bought a lot of them) and they always make her chuckle. A key reason I was elected: a lot of friends voted for me in two very small-town, low-voter-turnout elections.

After seventeen years of a very successful private real estate practice in town, the real estate market turned bad and I had to make a change, not just for the economics but because I was forced to go back into litigation when the market dried up. In a small town that means—nightmare of nightmares—matrimonial practice. Any lawyer who isn't a "shark," any lawyer who is troubled by watching spouses battle out every detail of their lives, realizes very quickly that no one wins in a divorce, and children *always* lose, no matter what the circumstances.

The absolute turning point came one night when I woke Taffy in the middle of the night, loudly proclaiming in the middle of a dream, "I FORGOT ORTHODONTURE!" I had startled her with this bizarre, middle-of-the-night *non sequitur*, but she calmed me down and asked if I remembered the dream. I did. A few weeks earlier, a twenty-something woman had come into my office from a local beauty parlor referral. She told me she was from the Midwest and had gone on a singles vacation, one of those with minimal nudity, and met her future husband there. He was a young Wall Streeter, and he had swept her off her (bare) feet. They were married three months later, and she was pregnant three weeks after that. He bought a house in Chappaqua and appeared to lose interest in her as her pregnancy advanced. She called him when she went into labor and he did not show up at the hospital. The following day after the baby was born, he appeared and handed her a card and said, "This is my lawyer. I do not want to be a father, and I do not want to be your husband. Have your lawyer call my lawyer," and walked out. I was now her lawyer, her banking adviser, and her psychologist, and I had to plan the divorce, along with the baby's life and needs for the next twenty-one years.

I called the husband's attorney, who worked at a large Wall Street firm, and all he said to me was, "You draft a separation agreement, and if it is not too over the top in favor of your client, my client will agree to it." I was now facing an awesome responsibility. I thought about all the usual things you put into an agreement: support, health care, division of assets, summer camp and preschool, tuition through college, and anything else I could possibly ask for. I sent the draft proposal to the attorney and the following night suffered my nightmare. I FORGOT ORTHODONTURE!

My wife saw how unhappy I was and asked me what I liked about my law practice. I declared that the only thing I liked was Thursday nights when I sat as Town Judge. Taffy, in her profound down to earth, sensible, we-can-do-it way, simply said, "Well then, let's get you elected as a full-time judge."

She sent me to the Democratic Party to find out how to get nominated, and she went to the library to learn how to run a campaign. I was registered as an Independent at the time, and the Democratic Party told me they had a waiting list of Jewish lawyers who wanted to be judges and to come back in five years. I came home crestfallen, and Taffy simply said, "Go to the Republican Party—you are registered as an Independent. See what they say." This suggestion of hers made sense from a practical point of view. The Republican Party thought I would be an ideal candidate since, being Jewish, I would balance their heavily Italian ticket. Knowledge of the law, reputation, and standing in the community have very little to do with political nominations, you see. Sadly, I believe this is the case throughout our judicial system.

I received the nomination to run for County Court judge from the Republican Party and was told to begin fund-raising. Strange rules for judges: you have to have cocktail parties where you are the guest of honor, but you are not allowed to see the guest list since it might look as if you would favor any attorney who contributed to your campaign. May I ask you, who else in this world *would* contribute? I was convinced that when I showed up to give my little speech, a speech that remained neutral on most issues—including the death penalty, abortion, and so forth—I would have to wear a blindfold so as not to recognize anyone when I shook their hand and thanked them for coming, Talk about a set of rules that make absolutely no sense!

As soon as you receive the Republican nomination, you are all but assured of the Conservative Party's as well. Shortly after that happened, I received a call from the chairman of the Right to Life Party. If you are not familiar, the Right to Life Party's platform is to be staunchly anti-abortion and opposed to stem cell research, euthanasia and more. The chairman asked me to meet him for lunch in White Plains and, as a courtesy, I agreed. At the lunch he told me how powerful his party was and how they could make or break a candidate's election. He then offered me the Right to Life Party nomination. As polite and as genuine as I could be, I told him that I would not accept his offer. He asked me for my reasons, and I told him that I would not accept a nomination from any one-issue party. In addition to that, if I accepted the nomination, I would be sending a message that I favored the ideology of the party endorsing me, and whether or not I did favor the ideology (which I did not), it would be a conflict of interest in my opinion if I ever had an abortion case appear before me. He was quite upset with me and lunch ended shortly after that. (I picked up the check.)

The Gannett newspapers invited me to be interviewed by their editorial board, and even though they had never, to the best of my knowledge, endorsed a Republican, I went. They asked a hundred questions of me and finished with, "Why didn't you take the Right to Life Party endorsement?" I told them what had happened and they just looked at me. One of the editors smiled and said, "You are a different kind of Republican candidate than we have ever had before us." I told them about the Democrats not wanting to nominate me. They laughed—and then the Gannett chain of newspapers endorsed me. If you want to look at a diverse set of endorsements, I was also endorsed by the National Organization for Women, the Affiliated Police Associations of Westchester County, the New York State Troopers PBA, the Westchester County Department of Public

Safety, the District Attorneys Association, the Police Conference of New York, the Police Emerald Society of Westchester, the Police Columbia Association of Westchester, the Suffolk County Police Pulaski Association, the Westchester Irish Committee, Local 32E Service Employees International Union, Local 664, United Auto Workers (UAW), the Westchester Coalition for Legal Abortion, the *Women's News*, and countless local organizations.

It was by no means a landslide election. I once again gave away pencil-gavels in the new campaign and to this day I have people asking me if I still have any to give them. I guess people make a lot of mistakes and need two erasers. In addition to a wonderful, passionate team of volunteers, my wife was my scheduler for events, my daughter Karen set up a train-station schedule so the commuters could meet me and we would hand out my campaign pamphlet and the pencils. My daughter Amy helped with everything and was my lucky charm whenever she came with me to a rally. After five months of grueling public appearances, including an annual Polish pig roast, a Jewish inquisition at various Temple meetings, an Italian Heritage Festival held at Kensico Dam in the central part of Westchester, and many many more it became very hard to keep smiling. At the end of one exhausting weekend, the last item on the list of scheduled appearances was the Cuban-American Caucus of Port Chester, in the southern part of the county. There were 7,500 Cuban American voters registered in Port Chester at that time, and I was the only candidate to show up. I speak enough Spanish to get by, and they insisted after my speech that I stay and have dinner with them. I won the election by less than five thousand votes, and so I thank Fidel Castro for chasing all those wonderful Cuban immigrants to Port Chester so that they could vote for me!

My campaign was six months long in total. It's amazing how little you are allowed to say as a judicial candidate. Usually,

Marion, my volunteer driver and the sister of my daughter Amy's best friend Suzanne, would get me to an event with five to fifteen minutes to spare. I would go up to the platform, be introduced, and then give a speech about all the qualifications that I had to be a judge. Then there would be a brief question-and-answer period, and then I would leave, and Marion would deliver me to my next stop – after offering her astute critique of my speech, of course. Marion knew everybody on the planet and would walk two steps in front of me and say loudly, "Assemblyman Smith, I want you to meet the judge," and I would walk up and say, "Hello, Assemblyman Smith." (Or, if I remembered their first name from the newspapers, I would use their first name.) "How is the family?" I cannot tell you how pleased they were that it appeared that I recognized them.

The first really surprising incident of my campaign happened at Kensico Dam. I had finished my speech, and was working the front row of the crowd as I was leaving. Thank goodness, I had more than just Marion with me. I shook hands with one voter who gripped my hand and pressed, "Are you one of those liberal judges who believe in abortion?" My protection for the day was a private detective and friend, Peter Tartaglia. He immediately came up to my side as I answered this guy with the usual pat answers: judges cannot express opinions about issues that might come before them, and my personal feelings have nothing to do with my decision-making from the bench. As I was finishing, he took a swing at me that never landed, since Pete had him on the ground before he finished swinging. Marion and another volunteer quickly escorted me out of there. Unless an assault has happened to you personally, you have no idea how you will react. I was willing to stand there and talk to the guy, but Pete saw something I didn't and reacted faster than I could have. There were not many incidents like that after Kensico, but it certainly put me on my guard.

By the time election night arrived, Dad was too ill to come to headquarters at Crabtree's Kittle House Inn in Chappaqua but Mom did, as did many friends and volunteers. It was a tense evening for me, since I was running against the former head of the Democratic Party, also Jewish. Dad was at home with a nurse and beyond being consumed with worry about his health; we missed having him there. When I won, we called him immediately with the results and he was so excited! My daughter Karen was studying abroad in Rome, Italy at the time, but at 3:00 in the morning she went to the pay phone at her dormitory and called to get the exciting results! My dear friend Chuck Banks (Charles G. Banks III) drove my mother home, and we all sat around and talked about how I was now going to leave my law practice and become a County Court judge and acting Supreme Court justice for Westchester County. It was, and still is, a very heady feeling, and, truthfully, I was a bit apprehensive; this was going to be a significant change in my life and my responsibilities.

My dad was very proud of me, and although he was still struggling with the effects of a stroke he had suffered, we would often talk about cases both before and after court. I loved having him in court before he became ill and would call him at home when he became bedridden as often as I could. He would never tell me what decision to make—he would just quietly add his thoughts to give me another viewpoint to consider. This became harder after the stroke as he was struggling with his speech. I miss his advice. I will always miss his advice. It was late December the year I was elected to County Court when his doctor called me and told me that he would not likely live until my swearing-in ceremony in late January. I called Administrative Judge Angelo Ingrassia and told him. He called me back later that day and said he had rounded up several judges who were on Christmas break and asked them to come to the courthouse in two days. Could I get my father there? I assured him that I could. We all met in my new chambers and shortly after, the ambulance arrived with my dad. Two court officers, a nurse, and my mother wheeled my dad in. He was clutching a bottle of champagne and said, "OK, let's get on with it so I can open the bubbly!" As Judge Ingrassia swore me in, it seemed to me that everyone was quietly crying. I know I was. Everyone wanted to talk to my dad, and he was great. He had trouble articulating all the things he wanted to say, and my mom explained that he was exhausted and she wanted to take him home. Mom called me a few days later saying she and Dad were talking about the swearing in and he was so happy for me he had cried—and a moment later he died. I will always think warm and kind thoughts toward you, Angelo, for what you did for my family and me. Thank you again. When I am lecturing to a large crowd, part of me looks out at the audience and imagines Dad there. So many happy Dad memories!

When I think back to moments Dad and I shared, I always remember the sage advice my rabbi gave me after Dad died. It was weeks after the funeral, and Rabbi Chaim Stern (author of *Gates of Prayer*, among others) came to the house to see how I was doing. I sat in the living room with him and told him how much I was hurting. He looked at me and asked, "What do you miss the most about your dad?" I instantly knew the answer, and said that I missed talking to him and receiving his always-brilliant advice. Rabbi Stern looked at me, and with a wise rabbinical smile on his face said, "You can talk to him as often as you like!" I have and sometimes I still do. I loved those two men.

A few months after I was elected and that guy had tried to hit me at Kensico Dam, I had a speaking engagement at the Crowne Plaza White Plains-Downtown hotel. I was at the courthouse getting ready to leave when my sergeant came in, and asked who I wanted to have accompany me for security. I told him he was being overly cautious, that this was the Westchester

County Bar Association meeting and that I did not need security. He disagreed, and we were arguing when a young attorney, Jim Scalise, came in and asked if I would like to walk over to the hotel with him. I looked at the sergeant and I decided that Jim would be my security, and after some cajoling the sergeant agreed. On the way to the hotel, Jim, a mild-mannered guy, asked me what he was supposed to do as security. I explained that I did not think any of the attorneys at the meeting would attack me and we laughed at the situation. We arrived at the hotel and headed for the ballroom. When we got there, a vice president of the Bar Association was there to greet us, to apologize, and to tell us that they were running a few minutes late, and that there was no anteroom, and would we mind waiting in the hallway a little while? So we waited.

A moment later the elevator doors opened, and a middle-aged, slightly stout woman emerged. She glanced at us and I knew immediately that she recognized me. Now, you must understand that I had by then met thousands of people while I was campaigning. She might have been a senator or a mayor or an attorney going to the meeting, or just a voter who had met me, but I did not recognize her.

She started walking quite purposefully toward us and Jim whispered to me, "What do I do?" I told him to relax. He edged in front of me. The closer she got, the more Jim moved in front of me. I then noticed a pen in his hand. Hell of a defensive weapon, but better than none, he must have thought. When she was three feet away, Jim and I were concerned but were trying to be politic. She looked at me and asked, "You are Judge Leavitt, aren't you?" Jim tensed. We both thought the next line was going to be something about how I had ruined her life or something like that. I answered that indeed I was Judge Leavitt.

She said, "I want to thank you. When you were Town Judge in Chappaqua, my son appeared before you. Three years ago, instead of putting him in jail for drug possession you sent him to rehabilitation and put him on probation. I want to tell you, he has successfully kicked drugs, his fiancé has come back to him, he has a good job and you are the person to thank!" Where the hell are the newspaper reporters when that sort of thing happens? I thanked her profusely, wished her every good fortune, and was then called into the bar meeting. I told them what had just happened and the anecdote was truly fortuitously timed.

The courthouse in White Plains is named after County Court Judge Richard Daronco, who was murdered by a disgruntled father who did not like the way Judge Daronco decided his daughter's matrimonial case. Judges get threats all the time, more about that later, but it is the most rewarding and challenging job I ever had. Every day brought a new challenge, and I had to be at my best constantly. I loved going to work every single morning.

There are many, many more campaign stories but perhaps I should save them just in case I write another book about how to—and how *not* to—run a campaign.

9

Court Officers: "You Have to Be On the Job 15 Years to Know"

Being a judge is the greatest job, even though you do have to give up certain constitutional rights and privileges. I told you that I loved the challenge of going to work every day to face new cases and situations, some mellow, some outright dangerous. I learned very quickly that the court officers assigned to a judge are the most underrated people in the courthouse. They are responsible for the operation of the courtroom, transporting prisoners back and forth, judges' safety, the public's safety, and more. The sergeant in charge is the key. When I was brand new to the job, I spoke to my first sergeant and let him know that I was not some pompous ass who thought he knew everything just because I had the title of *Judge*. He looked at me with steely eyes and said simply, "We'll see." Less than two months later I was sentencing a very bad dude who jumped on the defense table and leapt toward me. The sergeant had strategically placed one of his officers nearby and George, an exceptional court officer, caught him in midair and dropped him face-first on the floor. No one attacks a judge on George's watch! After all the commotion had died down, I asked the sergeant how he knew that something might happen and he looked at me and said, "You have to be on the job fifteen years to know!"

I sponsored a Christmas party for the court officers, clerks, and other staff my first year on the bench and each year thereafter, something I would have done whether or not they had saved me from that guy. After the first party, my sergeant came up to me and said, "You were right, Judge, you are not a pompous ass!" It made me feel good.

But that party got me into trouble with the administrative judge, who told me that judges just don't *do* that. They just take their law clerks and secretaries out to lunch, and I was embarrassing the rest of the judges (who did not make much effort to thank the court officers at holiday time). I responded that they were all welcome to share the cost of the luncheon with me, but unfortunately not one of them joined me in sponsoring the party. Six years later, a new administrative judge announced to me one November morning, "Do not plan your usual party. I am going to sponsor a party for all the staff." My sergeant came over to me at that first administrative judge's party, credited me with the change for the annual party, and thanked me for being "a regular guy." At that party, *every* court officer there made it a point to come over to my table and thank me, a gesture that did not go unnoticed by the other judges. I was the only judge asked to join the court officers at their annual golf holiday in Myrtle Beach, and I will always be proud of that. It doesn't take much to thank people who are often underappreciated, but it's something my parents taught me to do and that has become a central part of my personal code.

Let me get back to what you can and cannot do as a judge, in addition to the restrictions that your administrative judge places upon you, or *suggests*.

To give you the best idea of the restrictions on judges, take a look at the *Iowa Code of Judicial Conduct*. The *Iowa Code of Judicial Conduct* is a model code for the country. There are seven canons contained in the code:

1. A judge should uphold the integrity and independence of the judiciary.
2. A judge should avoid impropriety and the appearance of impropriety in all activities. (For example, if you go out to lunch with an attorney or attorneys who appear or have appeared before you, the rule is that you announce in a loud voice for all to hear, "Separate checks please!")
3. A judge should perform the duties of office impartially and diligently.
4. A judge may engage in activities to improve the law, the legal system, and the administration of justice. A judge once announced at summer judges' school that he was being honored for donating twenty-five years of service to the Boy Scouts. The administrative judge asked him if there was an admission price to the dinner. There was. Was there any profit in the price of the tickets for the Boy Scouts? Yes. "The Boy Scouts get one dollar per ticket."

"Then you cannot attend," the administrative judge told him, "since it is a fundraiser and you cannot use your judicial office to help raise funds." Several expletives later, the judge vowed to go anyway. This only goes to prove the adage if you do not want to hear an adverse answer to your question, do not ask it!

5. A judge should regulate extrajudicial activities to minimize the risk of conflict with judicial duties. (At an ethics class we all attended, a judge asked if he could still pass the collection plate at his church and was told no, since it would put pressure on the attorneys who attended to donate more. I wonder if that is still the rule.)

6. Be cautious about any compensation received for quasi-judicial and extra-judicial activities. (Are golf winnings a quasi-judicial activity? If so, I'm in trouble.)
7. A judge should refrain from political activity inappropriate to the judicial office (for example, a political party fundraiser). I laugh. How can a judge expect to be reelected if you do not participate? I never had that problem since I was going to retire after my ten-year term.

When I attended judges' school immediately after my election, the chief administrative judge was lecturing us on courtroom demeanor and voiced a concern about what he called judicial *humor*. "Some judges," he told us, "out of personal good nature, or out of a desire to break the tension that can develop in a courtroom, occasionally feel it appropriate to treat a captive audience to a display of wit. Sometimes it is appreciated by the audience, but sometimes not. Judges may underestimate the seriousness of the proceedings felt by the litigants, and misinterpret a judge's remarks. Without wishing to be a killjoy, I would caution against giving too much scope to your natural humor or high spirits when presiding in a courtroom."

Well, I've told you about my experience as a stand-up comedian. I never took my courtroom proceedings lightly, but I do believe that lightening the tension through an occasional (appropriate) witticism is a good thing for everyone. Being in court – as a potential juror, a defendant, or a witness – is a stressful experience.

In order to ease the tension of jury selection, I would always admonish the prospective jury pool that if they felt they were to be sequestered during the trial not to expect a five-star hotel. Because of budgetary constraints, I would tell them, a local (hopefully uninfested) roach motel is where they'd probably be sent. It brought a few laughs and a release of tension and let the jury see early on that I was probably human after all, or at least that I had a sense of humor. I believe it put them at ease and helped demystify any stress they felt about serving on a criminal case.

After my dad passed away, my mom thought it was her responsibility to come watch me in court. She knew that if Dad had lived he would be there as often as he could, and then we would have lunch and talk about the cases. Without being morbid or sad, I've frequently thought about how nice that would have been if Dad could have been there with Mom. But Mom was often there to do the very same thing.

Sometime after the attempted attack in the courtroom, she was visiting for the morning and when I adjourned the morning session she followed me through the back of the courtroom to my robing room. My sergeant that term was Mookie, and he accompanied me of course, and my mother stopped us just outside the courtroom, looked at me, and asked, "Where's George (her personal favorite of my court officers)?" I asked her why. This feisty little ninety-six-pound grandmother looked at us and said to Mookie, "I'm his mother. You know, and *they* know and, I need security to go to my car!" Mookie looked at me, and without a blink called for George, told him what to do, and George, who was two and a half times the size of my mom, said to her with a big smile, "Don't you worry, Mrs. Leavitt. I will take you to the car." She kissed me good-bye and said, "I'll call you when I am home safe and sound." How could you not love that moment? George later told me that my mom had given him a kiss good-bye, and she whispered to him, "Thank you, George, and take care of my son, please."

I cannot leave this chapter without telling you a little more about the sergeants who run courtrooms. They move sergeants around from judge to judge during each term of court, and it would always bring a smile to my face when certain sergeants were rotated into my courtroom. There are good sergeants and better sergeants. During the course of a calendar call day and especially during a trial, every so often a sergeant will approach the bench and point something out to me that I'd missed. It might be a relative of the defendant's glaring at a witness or at the jury, a member of the press too close to the jury box, or something that I had to deal with summarily. The better sergeants seemed to know when the jury needed a bathroom break or anything else that needed attention – including the very important times that a juror might need to be dismissed for misconduct. I was and am still grateful to those men and women who help keep our courtrooms running smoothly and safely.

10

The Nature of Evidence: "I Did Not Know You Could Do That!"

I WOULD LIKE to spend a little time giving you a thumbnail understanding of our legal system. This understanding is essential to learning about our court structure. As you likely know, the US government, on both state and federal levels, is divided into three branches:

- The legislative branch, which *creates* the laws. (I will not be writing about them.)
- The executive branch, which *enforces* the laws. (I will not be writing about them, either.)
- The judicial branch, which *interprets* the laws. (I will be writing about them. You guessed it!)

Here is a common misconception: judges create new laws where none existed before. Not exactly right! But judges *are* asked on an almost daily basis to conduct hearings to determine, for example, if a new scientific test should be admitted as reliable.

During a case I had early in my time as a County Court trial judge, the prosecution asked one of the two victims, "Can you tell the jury what happened in your own words, Ms. Robbins?"

She was an attractive, divorced, thirty-four-year-old single mother and a schoolteacher. "I was sleeping in my apartment," she began. "It was around two-thirty in the morning when something woke me. At first I thought it was my daughter, Caroline, but then this young black man appeared right next to my bed. He was wearing a black ski mask." She paused.

"What happened next?"

"He pointed a knife at my face and said that if I didn't do whatever he told me he would cut my kid's mother fu*king throat! I started to struggle, but he held me down and slapped me hard across the face several times. I started to cry. He hit me again and said, "Do you really want your kid to die?" I stopped struggling and he forced me to put his penis in my mouth, and after a while he raped me." After that he left.

"Would you recognize the man who beat you and raped you if you saw him again?" the prosecution continued.

"I think so, but he had a mask on. I am pretty sure I knew his voice as someone I had seen and spoken to in the neighborhood grocery store."

"Did he wear a condom?"

"Objection," the defense attorney interrupted. "Leading the witness!"

I overruled the objection. "You may answer the question."

"NO," she said forcefully.

"To your knowledge, did he leave any semen on your bed or on you?"

"I saw a small stain on the sheets," she said, "but as I learned later, I then did everything wrong. I went in to check on Caroline and then went into the shower. I must have scrubbed for over an hour and then I used a douche. I just wanted to wash him off of me. Then I called the police."

The same perpetrator attacked a second woman less than a month later, within three blocks of the first rape. This victim was also a single mother, a young widow. She also had a young child sleeping in the next room. Her testimony was almost identical to the first victim's. She described the attacker as wearing a black ski mask, same approximate height and weight, same threats to kill her child, same knife in her face, same hitting her in the face, same forced oral intercourse, and then rape. This victim was so traumatized that she flatly stated that she could not identify her attacker. Unlike the first victim, this one immediately called the police and went to the hospital, where she had what is called a "rape kit" performed; a series of examinations and tests to determine the extent of the physical assault and recover any DNA evidence (i.e., hair, blood, or semen) the attacker might have left. The rape kit recovered a sizable sample of semen.

The police were able to identify the attacker from the women's descriptions. Before they arrested him, they went to the district attorney with the evidence they had. They produced the written reports, the sheet with the semen stain on it, and the rape kit, but the district attorney questioned them about whether they had probable cause to arrest the suspect. The definition of probable cause is, "A reasonable amount of suspicion supported by circumstances sufficiently strong enough to justify a reasonable person to believe that certain facts are true." The DA needed more.

The process of DNA testing was not as exact a science at that time (early1990s). Very few states had recognized DNA evidence as a reliable scientific tool. The case looked very weak. The DA went to the judge on duty and asked for a "blood order" to force the suspect to give a sample of blood to test against the stain on the sheet, since the trial judge had said that there was not enough of an identification in the second rape to justify the probable cause standard. The judge said he would grant the order, however, to test against the stain on the sheet in the first rape. The police picked up the suspect and brought him to the hospital, and a nurse took a sample of his blood.

On *Law & Order* or *CSI,* results are obtained between commercials, but in real life it generally takes a great deal longer; it can be weeks for the laboratory to make their determinations. In this case, they contacted the DA and told her that the stain on the bed-sheet from the first rape was too degraded to give a conclusive result. The DA then came to me, since I was then the judge that was assigned to the second case, and asked me if they could use the suspect's blood sample to test against the rape kit sample. I asked the DA to show me the probable cause in the second rape and she admitted that she did not have probable cause, but since we already had his blood, couldn't we use it anyway? Hard decision. Although there was no statute, case law, or precedent that would allow me to say yes, justice was not going to be served by letting this suspect walk free.

It was agonizing for a judge. I remember my dad (who also practiced law and then became a small claims court judge himself) telling me, "Hard cases make bad law! This is a tough case and it has unique circumstances." Dad never gave me the answers; he pointed me in new directions. How would I find the path to justice for these two victims? I decided to allow the results into evidence.

I conducted the hearings and then the trial of this multiple rape defendant. It was the first time that DNA evidence was used in the prosecution of a rape case in my jurisdiction. I heard scientific testimony in the pretrial hearings and ruled that the DNA testing was scientifically reliable and could be used. My rationale for allowing the results of the DNA tests was that since the state already had his blood sample from the first rape, it should be equated to a mug shot or a fingerprint since it required no further invasion of the defendant's body and his blood sample could be tested against the rape kit. It was an absolute match. The defendant was found guilty on all charges. The jury was out less than two hours. I sentenced him to two consecutive sentences in state prison.

A Latin phrase was drummed into our heads at Fordham Law School: *lex de futuro judex de praeterito*, which means *the law provides for the future; the judge for the past*. Not so fast! I've always wanted to prove that wrong.

In life, there are times we have to stretch our imaginations and come up with new theories to justify doing what we know is the right thing to do. That rape case, after all the appeals had been decided, became the law. Currently, a hearing does not necessarily need to be conducted before trial. DNA evidence is considered so reliable that it is almost automatic that it can be introduced into evidence. And this is just one example of judges - and not the legislative branch - creating law where there was none before.

Judges also become creative when the state of the law does not meet the state of the times. A judge may have to render a decision not supported by any existing law—i.e. cell phone abuses. I am sure some of you have all received some of these fraudulent calls and Internet schemes. When a judge rules on a subject that is not yet codified law, it will be appealed and the case will eventually reach the highest court in the state. If it is affirmed, the legislature will probably take note and someone will introduce a bill codifying the decision and making it into "black letter [officially codified] law."

Now, I've tried to convey that the political hue and cry that "judges should not be activists" is often just rhetoric. Much like the US Constitution, an ever-evolving document (through Amendments), our current laws are also an ever-changing beast, and it needs judges with wise minds and guiding hands to manage it, define it, and, yes, to change it! I think it's important to discuss the impact judges have on the law, and it's especially important when it comes to crimes of violence. The double rape case that I found a solution to is but the proverbial tip of the iceberg.

I think you need to know a bit more about rape. Rape is essentially an act of power and dominance. Rape is a crime even if you know the person who raped you. A rapist can be a boyfriend, a fiancé, a nurse, a husband, a father, a coworker, or a boss. Even if the victim doesn't fight back, but did not consent to the act, it is still rape and still a crime. Even if you were drinking, taking drugs, given drugs, or unconscious it is still rape and still a crime if you did not consent. Anyone can be a rape victim—men and women, children, and the elderly. Between 50 and 70 percent of all rapes occur within the context of a romantic relationship, and over half of those rapes occur in the victim's home. Due to the victims' fear or embarrassment, rape is one of the most underreported crimes in our country. And it gets worse: less than 50 percent of rapes are reported, and only 2 percent of those reported are convicted. Finally, the vast majority of those convicted only serve half their sentences. You begin to see why judges take a particular interest in those types of cases that come before us. We develop a particular sensitivity to victims, while always striving to be fair and impartial. It's a difficult balancing act.

Rape is a difficult crime to prove. In several states, corroboration is still required. This means that you need a witness other than the victim to prove that the rape occurred. In other states, you must prove bodily injury or a struggle between the victim and his or her attacker. On the other hand, in a robbery case, a person only has to tell the police that someone pushed him and took his wallet, and robbery is considered as serious a felony as rape. Most states require physical evidence of recent sexual intercourse, which means that the victim has to undergo a physical examination within twenty-four hours of the assault (the afore-mentioned "rape kit.")

If the victim does report the rape, here is a brief profile of what a typical victim might endure:

- After reporting the facts to the first-responding police officer, the victim has to go to a hospital and repeat the same facts for a nurse or doctor, and undergo an intrusive examination using a rape kit to search for semen, hairs, fibers, blood, and saliva.
- While in the hospital, the victim must wait for a police detective and recount the rape a third time in much more detail.
- When the victim is released from the hospital, he or she then has to go to the police station and give a written statement to the police, recounting the rape a *fourth* time.
- The victim will then be called to local court for a preliminary hearing with the defendant there (assuming the victim knows the attacker and hasn't had to go to a lineup or other identification procedure), and will have to give testimony about the rape so that a judge can decide whether or not to hold the case for the grand jury.
- The victim must then appear at the grand jury. While there is no cross-examination, the victim must tell the story yet again and hope that they issue an indictment.
- The victim may be required to testify at hearings before the trial to ascertain if the identification procedure was fair, if there was one.
- Most traumatically of all, the victim also must appear for the trial, testify, and, in most states, be cross-examined at

length and asked repeatedly if it was the victim him or herself who enticed the defendant. In some jurisdictions, the victim may be asked about his or her sexual history.

And remember: only about 2 percent of rapes lead to convictions.

I had a particularly ugly rape case that was about to go to trial. We had finished all the motion practice and concluded all the hearings. We had not yet selected the jury, but that was the next step. The DA asked my court clerk Lisa if she could speak to me in the robing room. I agreed, but only with the defendant's attorney present. They came in and the DA immediately asked if he could speak to me *ex parte* (alone). By this time in my tenure, almost every attorney who appeared before me trusted my judgment and knew that I would not let anything improper happen, so the defendant's attorney agreed.

The DA told me that the victim was nine years old. Her mother was waiting in the empty jury room with her daughter and the mother had pleaded with the DA to talk to me. When I sent for the defendant's attorney, and after I told him the situation, he said he had no objection to my speaking to the mother.

I went with my court officer to the jury room. After saying hello, I suggested that the officer take the little girl to my robing room and get her a soda or something else that would keep her calm and comfortable. He was reluctant to leave me alone, but I told him I had no fear of the girl's mother, but he insisted on having a female court officer stay in the room with us. When her daughter left the room, this distraught mother looked at me and told me that under no circumstances was she going to allow her child to testify, to go into that courtroom and have to go through that nightmarish scene again. After the child was released from the hospital following the rape, she entered counseling. The mother described the ordeal her daughter had endured in going to the police station to identify her attacker. After that, the girl had had to testify at the grand jury. The mother described how after each time her daughter had to go through statements, she had to spend hours just holding her child, and that the girl now had to sleep with her every night while her husband slept on the sofa.

I told her that we had to try the case and stop this defendant from harming other children. I promised her that I would keep her daughter out of the courtroom and she could testify in a private room via closed-circuit television. We spoke for a long time, and afterward, she simply looked at me and said, "I don't care if you put *me* in jail. I will not put her through this again!" I asked her to wait and returned to my robing room. Armed with this information I called both attorneys in and simply told them to go conference somewhere and try to come back to me with a plea deal that I could stomach.

Fifteen minutes later, the attorneys returned and the defendant's attorney looked me straight in the eye and said, "My client wishes to plead guilty to a slightly reduced charge and the DA agrees to recommend a sentence of five to fifteen years in state prison." I agreed, and we went into the courtroom and took his guilty plea. I returned to the jury room and told the mother what had happened. She started to cry and thanked me over and over. When I went home that day, I had this mixed feeling of whether or not I had done the right thing. Should I have forced the girl to tell the story one more time and send this monster away for a very long time, or save the girl from painful further testimony and give her and her family the beginnings of closure? These are not the stories you read about in the media, because judges don't tend to talk about them.

The US Department of Justice statistics in 2004 reported that there were 247,000 rapes or sexual assaults in this country and 4,300 resulted in pregnancy. These figures do not include victims under the age of twelve. Eighty percent of rape victims are white. The highest percentages of victims in minority groups are American Indians and Alaskan natives. In a recent study by the US Department of Health and Human Services, it was reported that 44 percent of child rapes involve children under the age of eighteen, and 15 percent are under the age of twelve.

The following is a profile of a typical rapist. The average age is thirty-one. 52% of rapists are white and of them, 22% are married. In 33% of rapes, the rapist is intoxicated, 30% with alcohol, 3% with illegal drugs. Only 7% of rapists use a weapon: 2% use a gun, 5% use a knife. Rapists are more likely to be serial criminals rather than serial rapists.

I know that I am spending a lot of time on the issue of rape, but I have had hundreds of discussions with my family about the injustice of this crime and its aftermath. During such discussions, my mom would have to find some pretext to leave the room and do something else. It seemed to be too much for her to even listen to. I respected that but still I sought the advice of my dad, wife, and sister. Karen and I discussed the problem of sexual assaults at her school, Duke University. No one knew how to separate themselves from the nightmares, except to keep trying to help me determine how to do the right and the just thing.

Now that I have painted this grim and shocking picture of a horrible and devastating crime, I have to tell you that there are people out there that do try to achieve justice. Taking another look at the struggle that judges go through to do the best for these victims will give you an idea of the tremendous burden we face as jurists, and will hopefully have you thinking a few kinder thoughts about the job we do.

This balancing act doesn't just apply to judges. It starts with law enforcement. There are so many dedicated policemen and policewomen out there who know the law and how hard it is for rape victims to come forward – and how hard it is to get a conviction in rape cases.

But there are those people who really try to make a difference.

The time has come to tell you about Monk! When it comes to rape, a subject on which I will move on from shortly, I would be remiss if I did not relate this to you. In order to do that, I must take you back to the district attorney's office in Brooklyn. The newbies in the office had passed the bar exam but were still assigned to "ride homicide" every so often. This time, the phone rang at around 11:00 p.m. The call was from a detective nicknamed Monk who worked in a police precinct in Bedford-Stuyvesant (a notoriously bad place at the time). He had called me directly, which was unusual. I do not know how he got my number or knew that I was the duty ADA. He told me that he needed an assistant district attorney to take statements on a particularly nasty rape case. He stated that the victim was at the precinct and could and would identify the rapist. He told me they had already arrested him and were waiting for a DA. I notified the District Attorney's driver—he picked me up, and the stenographer and we went to the precinct.

As usual, we went to the captain's office and the stenographer, Richie, set up his machine. Monk, by the way, had a huge reputation for being not only rough around the edges but for pushing the envelope whenever he had to, in order to get a conviction. The word in the DA's office was always to be careful when working with Monk. Not that he was a bad guy, just that you should be careful. He was also a bruiser, over six feet three inches and very muscular. *Intimidating* was a compliment.

Monk then brought a sixteen-year-old girl into the office. She was a light skinned, slim African-American girl who was very pretty despite all the damage the rapist had done to her face with his fists. I took her complete statement and made sure that Monk had a female officer drive her home and stay with her as long as necessary. Monk then said that he had no corroboration for the crime and that the rapist was a repeat offender. We looked at him and asked why he bothered to get us to come here since the rapist knew the ropes and probably wouldn't talk to us. Monk then looked me in the eye and said the most prophetic thing he might have said, "Trust me!" You know the expression *a shiver went up my spine*? That was an understatement. We were speechless, which for me – as you surely realize by now – is unheard of.

Monk walked out of the room and the two of us waited. A minute or two went by. Then the door to the captain's office opened and the accused, let's call him "Leroy," entered. His hands were cuffed in front of him and were chained to his waist, and he had ankle chains on, which was highly unusual for the inside of a police precinct. Monk followed him in and directed him to sit in a chair directly in front of the captain's desk.

"This is the DA," said Monk. "He's the one you get to talk to." I looked at Monk and then at Leroy, and I was sure that Leroy was not going to talk to me. He was another big bruiser of a guy, with scrapes on his knuckles and a king-size attitude. I began my ritual, introducing myself and pointing to the stenographer, and then began reciting his Miranda rights (which you are surely familiar with, at least from television). I had gotten to the second sentence, "You have a right to remain silent..." when Monk interrupted and asked if we could wait a minute—he would be right back. I signaled Richie to stop, and we watched in utter surprise as Monk walked out of the room and closed the door behind him!

Being left alone in the room with Leroy and Richie was more than a little frightening. I was still fresh out of law school, and not having a clue as to what was happening, I just sat there, pretending to write some very important information on the pad in front of me. Less than two minutes elapsed before the phone on the captain's desk rang, and since I knew that at this hour the call was not for the captain, I picked up the receiver. It was Monk. In a hushed tone, he asked me, "Can you step out for a second?" I am not sure what possessed me to leave Richie alone in the room with Leroy, but I got up and left.

Monk was in the outer office and he asked, "Do you want a cup of coffee?"

For anyone who has ever had the misfortune of drinking station house coffee, you might recall a taste similar to burned rubber or hot motor oil, so I politely declined and asked what the hell was going on. Very quietly and confidentially he said, "Trust me." There were those fateful words again.

I went back into the office, sat down, and resumed my Miranda rights reading. "If you cannot afford an attorney..." Suddenly, the door burst open and Monk walked in with his hands full of stuff. He placed a rectangular piece of glass on the edge of the desk, and then put a blank fingerprint card next to the glass. He produced a roller and a jar of fingerprint ink, the old kind that took days to wash off. He rolled ink onto the glass. Monk looked at Leroy, and barked, "Stand up Leroy!" Leroy instantly obeyed. "Take your prick out and roll it on the ink and then on the card!" Leroy looked dumbstruck but complied, and Monk looked at him and said, "I bet you didn't know that we can now match prick prints." He handed Leroy two paper towels to clean himself with, took the ink, glass, roller, fingerprint card, and walked out.

Stunned, but still trying to act professionally, I said, "Statement resumes." This time, when the phone rang, I just walked out of the office. Monk stood there with two other detectives, quietly laughing themselves blue. Monk asked us to stall for a couple of minutes. I did, but then went back in and resumed the interview once again; once again the door burst open. Monk burst in clutching two fingerprint cards. He shouted, "Your prick print matched her pussy print! We got you now!" Leroy looked at him and then at me and said, "I did not know you could do that!" and proceeded to give us a complete confession.

In consideration of my younger readers, I will not relate what Ed Panzarella had to say to me the next day when he reviewed the report.

11

A History of Juries: "Not to Accuse an Innocent Man or Spare a Guilty One"

I started to tell you about the power of judges to change the law, but now I want you to understand the power of the judges when it comes to the jury system and jury trials. The power of the judiciary is immense. You need a primary understanding of the jury system to see clearly how the system is not as even-handed as one would like to think it is.

In 1787, the members of the first Continental Congress of the United States preserved the right to trial by jury, ensuring that they and future generations would be judged by their fellow citizens and not by the government. This doctrine is codified in the Sixth Amendment in the Bill of Rights, which states that in a criminal prosecution, an accused person has the right "to a speedy and public trial by an impartial jury, and every defendant shall be informed of all charges against him."

The idea of juries is so closely interwoven with that of the courts that for most members of the American public, the image of a courtroom means a judge in a black robe, a prosecuting attorney and a defense attorney, and the rows of twelve men and women looking on and listening closely to the testimony as it unfolds.

The Magna Carta of 1215 held several references to trials and juries. It stated in part that juries shall consist of "honest men of the neighborhood." By the end of the fifteenth century, a jury was not a body of witnesses, but a body that heard the testimony of witnesses and unanimity became necessary to convict a defendant in a criminal trial.

I used to talk to my grandfather Pop (my mother's stepfather), who was born and raised in London—about England, English common law, the monarchy, justice, and fairness. He was a wonderful, soft-spoken man who always had the same advice for me when I would ask him about a big decision I had to make – legal or otherwise. Should I go to the movies on a date or take her to Coney Island? Save my money or buy something I desired but didn't need? He would put a work-worn hand on my shoulder and say, "Everything in moderation, my boy, will get you through life." His was the voice I heard whenever I was faced with a tough emotional question.

My daughter Amy has also told me that Pop's "everything in moderation" admonition has helped her through many a difficult situation. She just takes a deep breath and thinks about what Pop said and works her way to a reasonable solution to the problem. Sound easy? It's a great deal of simple common sense when you think of the big picture and realize that things are really not that bad.

There are two types of jurors: petit and grand. Petit jurors are sworn to hear evidence in civil and criminal trials and render a verdict. Petit jurors are so designated because fewer people sit on a petit jury than on a grand jury. Petit jurors can be called to serve for as little as one day. Grand jurors on the other hand usually serve for at least one month intermittently and may serve for much longer periods of time, sometimes exceeding a year.

The grand jury has a duty to receive evidence presented by the state, and find bills of indictment in cases where they are satisfied that there is probable cause to believe a crime has been committed and that the defendant has committed it. Usually, grand juries are composed of twenty-three members and at least twelve of them must be present at each session before a grand jury may transact business.

Grand juries, as you may not realize, are a prosecutor's own private power machine. One of the earliest concepts of grand juries dates back to Ancient Greece, where the Athenians used an "accusatory body" (to put someone on trial). In early Britain, the Saxons also used something similar to a grand jury system. From the year 978 to 1016, one of the "Dooms Laws" stated that for each one hundred men, twelve were to be named to act as an accusing body. They were simply cautioned "not to accuse an innocent man or spare a guilty one."

The state attorney (or district attorney or state prosecutor, depending upon the jurisdiction) has tremendous control over what the grand jury does. When I was in the Brooklyn DA's office and did my several month stint as a grand jury assistant, the first thing I was told was that the grand jury would indict a bagel if I wanted it to.

A grand jury is a secret proceeding behind closed doors. The defendant has no right to be present, unless he or she wishes to testify, and then can have an attorney present who cannot participate in the proceedings. The prosecutor introduces just enough evidence for the grand jury to decide if "the suspect is probably the person who did this act." Maybe not as easy as the indictment of a bagel, but still pretty hard for the prosecutor to lose. Not every state uses the grand jury system; only about half, but every federal criminal charge requires an indictment.

I have observed district attorneys "over-indict" defendants to play to the press and to influence public opinion. This happens when the facts may technically justify charging murder but the more realistic charge would be manslaughter, since it would be obvious that there was a totally viable defense to murder.

Please understand that this is my opinion only. Unfortunately, this use of prosecutorial power has led to many abuses by a district attorney. The Duke University lacrosse players, for example, were indicted on very shaky evidence. As I mentioned, my daughter Karen went to Duke, and believe me – if any male students there were guilty of sexual assault, I would be the first to say they should be sent away. But the charges ended up being unfounded. Of course, it was during an election year, so perhaps the DA felt that he had to look tough since that was what the public wanted.

There are times that a judge is challenged to enforce a new law. In 1996, the first test of Megan's Law in New York State came before me. Megan's Law – which allows communities to track the whereabouts of convicted sex offenders – was enacted in New Jersey in 1994, after seven-year-old Megan Kanka was killed by an offender who had two prior convictions for sex offenses. Shortly after, New York enacted a statute that was similar to but not as sweeping as the New Jersey statute.

The statute was about two years old when the case came before me for sentencing on January 29, 1996. The defendant was Joseph Rossillo, who was fifty-nine at the time. He had been convicted of the statutory rape of a sixteen-year-old relative of his. The District Attorney's office offered him a plea deal with a sentence of five years probation because the rape victim had strenuously pleaded with the DA not to have to testify. I had taken his guilty plea and sentenced him to the five years probation he pleaded to, and then ordered that he be listed in the state's directory of sex offenders.

By itself, this would not have raised a lot of eyebrows, given the widespread public support of Megan's Law, but this case went a bit further. At his plea, he admitted that he first raped the victim when she was eleven years old. I immediately ordered that he be electronically monitored under house arrest, as he had been convicted of third-degree rape and was determined to be a "Level Two" risk.

What turned this case into one of unusual notoriety was that I also ordered him to relocate from his home as quickly as possible since he lived about one hundred yards from an elementary school. *USA Today* ran an article about him; *48 Hours* and *The Montel Williams Show* tried unsuccessfully to book him. Rossillo was listed in the directory for ten years according to the time periods established by the Statute.

Now, it may sound like a no-brainer for a judge to impose a statute enacted by his state's legislature, but since it was the first case in New York heard under the statute, I had to examine the language and determine if in my opinion it was unduly harsh, and whether or not there were constitutional questions I had to review. This may not sound like the judge's job, but a judge would be a fool if he did not review newly enacted legislation that he or she has to deal with.

In the next chapter, I will discuss juries and the interesting and unique powers that they have. As Americans, we have both a legal obligation and the privilege to serve on jury duty for trials of fellow citizens, and I hope that what I have learned and will share with you will help you understand both how juries are chosen and how best to serve your time on "jury duty."

12

Juries Today: "The Jury's Responsibility Is to Deliver Justice"

Jury nullification occurs when a jury returns a verdict of not guilty, despite its belief that the defendant is indeed guilty of the violation charged. The jury in effect *nullifies* a law that it believes is either immoral or wrongly applied to the defendant whose fate they are charged with deciding.

The first recorded case of jury nullification was that of William Penn and William Mead in England in 1670. The jurors refused to convict these two Quaker activists, who had been charged with unlawful assembly. The judge refused to accept a verdict other than "guilty" and ordered the jurors to resume their deliberations without food or drink or toilet facilities for four days. When the jurors persisted in their refusal to convict, the court fined them and jailed them until the fines were paid. On appeal, the Court of Common Pleas ordered the jurors released, holding that they could not be punished for their verdict.

Jury nullification was introduced into America in 1735 in the trial of John Peter Zenger, printer of the *New York Weekly Journal.* Zenger repeatedly attacked Governor William Cosby of New York in his journal, violating the seditious libel law, which prohibited criticism of the king or his appointed officers, including governors. The attacks became sufficient to bring Zenger to trial. He clearly was guilty of breaking the law, which held that even true statements could be libelous. However, Zenger's lawyer, Andrew Hamilton, addressed the jury, arguing that the court's law was outmoded. Hamilton contended that falsehood was the principle thing that makes a libel. It took the jury only a few moments to nullify the law and declare Zenger not guilty. Since that case, truth has been an absolute defense in libel cases.

What powers do judges have when it comes to a jury verdict? Can judges overrule juries?

When I sat as a judge in lower court, the prosecutor brought a case to trial for endangering the welfare of a minor. Because the charge was a misdemeanor, there was only a six-person jury. A couple had hired a babysitter for their infant, a baby not yet able to walk, and when they tried to call the sitter later in the evening to check on things, there was no answer. They kept trying and finally called the police. When the police arrived, they could see the babysitter through a window sleeping on the couch, but could not awaken her by banging on the door and yelling as loudly as they could. They forced the door open and discovered that she was incredibly intoxicated.

Luckily, the baby was fine and had suffered no injuries. I charged the jury on the appropriate statute. They decided that even though the law stated that the babysitter had not met the legal requirements to have committed the crime of endangering the welfare of the baby, they decided to disregard the law and found the babysitter guilty, because they were so incensed by her conduct. Despite the jury's intention, and for the first and only time in my career, I set aside the verdict based on the law. Yes, judges can indeed set aside a guilty verdict, but have no power over a not-guilty one. I took a lot of heat over that dismissal, which went against all popular feelings in town, but I was bound to apply the law, not bend to an emotional public sentiment.

In 1902, Oliver Wendell Holmes stated, "The jury has the power to bring a verdict in the teeth of both law and fact." Harlan Stone, twelfth chief justice of the Supreme Court, said in 1941: "The law itself is on trial quite as much as the cause which is to be decided." (Harlan Stone is the jurist for whom Columbia Law School's Harlan Fiske Stone Scholar award is named, the award my brother Dik won when he was a law student there. I told you he was brilliant!)

If juries have the power to nullify, shouldn't they be told so? That's a good question. And why is this so important to judges? Judges have worried that informing jurors of their power to nullify will lead to jury anarchy, with jurors following their own sympathies. They suggest that informing jurors of their power to nullify will increase the number of hung juries.

Jury nullification has had both positive and negative applications. The negative ones include notorious cases in which all-white Southern juries in the 1950s and 60s refused to convict white supremacists for killing blacks despite overwhelming evidence of guilt. As a result of these cases, there is a practice among judges in their instructions when they charge the jury, that the judge determines the *law* and the jury is limited to only determine the *facts*. Such an instruction is misleading and diminishes the total province of the jury, which is to protect the defendant in cases where the jury feels he or she deserves their intervention.

The problem with the afore-mentioned all-white juries was not in jury nullification, but in jury selection. The jury was not representative of the community's population, and could therefore not provide a fair trial.

In one controversial case that I tried, the Westchester County District Attorney had pursued an indictment against a teenager for murder. The following facts were developed at trial.

The teenager's family, the Minotts, had moved from the Bronx to Mount Vernon to seek a better life. The first week in school, 17-year-old Hopeton Minott got into a fistfight with another boy. The hall monitors stopped the fight and took both boys to be disciplined. They were sent to the guidance counselor, who told them to return on Monday morning after their first class, and in the meantime to stay out of trouble.

That Monday, on his way to the guidance counselor's office, the boy and four of his friends jumped Hopeton in the hallway. They were beating him, and one of the boys pulled out a knife and started stabbing Hopeton. He was cut on his face and his hand but managed to wrestle the knife away from his attacker. The five attackers then backed away from him—and in those few seconds, Hopeton ran several steps toward the boy he thought had produced the knife, Shebuel Jackson, and reached out to stab him. Three blows went into Jackson's neck and pierced his carotid artery. Jackson bled to death minutes later. There was an indication in the trial testimony that the deceased Jackson *was* the one who pulled the knife and started stabbing Minott. Even if Jackson had been the attacker, it was a tragic loss of life.

Was this a case of self-defense or manslaughter or acting in the heat of the moment? The District Attorney, as I stated, had indicted him for murder. I tried that case, and during deliberations the jury sent me multiple notes asking for me to explain the self-defense statute. The trouble that judges experience charging a jury is that they must stick with the language of the statute, and cannot try to explain it in easier terms. The self-defense statute in New York is difficult to understand when read to someone. There was one phrase in particular that had the jury troubled. The statute states in part,

> Sec.35.15 sub 2. A person may not use deadly physical force upon another person under circumstances specified in subdivision one unless: (a) The actor reasonably believes that such other person is using or about to use deadly physical force. Even in such case, however, the actor may not use deadly physical force if he or she knows that *with complete personal safety, to oneself and others he or she may avoid the necessity of doing so by retreating* [emphasis added]...

Did Hopeton commit murder? Was this a crime that he had planned? Did he have more than seconds to decide what to do? The jury sent me a note with the verdict, telling me they had found the defendant not guilty of murder - contrary to the statute - but had found him guilty of a lesser charge on the technical aspects of the manslaughter statute. They stated afterward that they had done this only because they felt they had to follow the law as I had charged it, regarding Hopeton's "duty to retreat," and would I please be as lenient as the law would allow in sentencing the defendant? It was the first and only time in my career as a judge that a jury sent me a note all but apologizing for their verdict.

This was probably the most controversial sentencing I ever had. There was no doubt in my mind what had happened from listening to the testimony in the courtroom. One of the major objections I have to the media is the knee-jerk reaction they have to situations, without direct knowledge of what really happened.

Almost every report on that case was written by someone who was not present to hear the testimony.

When the jury found Minott not guilty of murder, but guilty of manslaughter, I understood the dilemma I was facing. I could sentence him as an adult and send him to state prison or treat him as a youthful offender and sentence him to probation. He had no previous criminal record of any kind. There were two tragedies here: a dead boy and a boy whose life would never be the same. I chose the most difficult and controversial path and sentenced him to five years probation.

Westchester County District Attorney Jeanine Pirro and the media had a field day with judge-bashing me. The *Daily News* referred to me as a "junk judge," but coming from that paper I considered it a compliment. The newspapers reported that Jeanine accused me of "being the trouble with the criminal justice system." I knew the slings and arrows that would be hurled at me and warned my family and friends about what was about to happen. I received as many hate letters as supportive letters. I was vilified in the press and congratulated by the people who told me how much courage it must have taken for me to do what I did. I know I did the right thing and I know that I would do it again if faced with the prospect of bad press or doing what I considered was the correct thing: serving justice as I believed it should have been served.

Do not get me wrong. I have no animosity for the DA. The district attorney's office in my jurisdiction did more for victims' rights than any of the previous district attorneys had ever done. There are just times that I disagreed with some of the decisions that Jeanine Pirro (or others in her office) made, but that is just my personal opinion.

Judges have a lot of tough decisions to make and sometimes they have to agonize over a case and ignore the media. Juries have been faced with this type of difficult choice for a long time.

I truly believe that for the vast majority of cases, juries do the right thing. Let's look at some of the hard choices juries have made throughout American history.

In the 1920s, jury nullification was a major factor in liquor law trials, when juries were refusing to convict those who broke these laws. This effectively led to the repeal of Prohibition. In Kentucky, juries often refused to convict anyone under the marijuana laws. Some other examples of nullification include Mayor Marion Barry of Washington for drug use, Oliver North for his role in the Iran-Contra affair, and Bernhard Goetz for his assault in a New York City subway. In all the above examples, juries refused to hand down convictions in these cases because they thought that the laws were wrong, or that what they saw as justice had to be done. Law is all we have to level the playing field.

Victor Hugo, in his book *Les Misérables,* highlighted the difference between justice and the law when he said, "The jury's responsibility is to deliver justice, not to uphold the law."

And then there's O.J. Simpson.

I desperately wanted to be the judge in that case because I felt they had a judge (Judge Lance Ito) who did not want to make any decisions. Almost every time the "Dream Team" (Johnnie Cochran, et al.) moved for a mistrial, Judge Ito reserved decision and usually waited for a few days before deciding on the motion. What the hell was he getting paid for? Make a decision on the spot! That's what judges do! (He does have a nice hourglass collection though.) For those of you who did not get to read the entire transcript of the trial and were just angry or upset by the verdict, let me set a few things right. The jury heard a lot of scientific testimony that contradicted the police in several respects. The famous glove was one, but to me when I heard the testimony about the bloody sock that could not possibly have blood on both sides as the police stated they found it,

I felt the way the jury did: police overkill, and doubts raised in my mind. I am not advocating that O. J. was innocent, but when you find the police lying about some of the evidence, well, you start having doubts about the case.

Finally, let's take a look at how the jury system evolved and how each jury comes to be comprised of those who are selected.

In 1968, Congress passed the Jury Selection and Service Act, a law that provided that the jury pool consist of all eligible voters, and that names be selected as needed on a random basis, like a lottery. Some people were to be excused from jury service for reasons such as blindness, inability to speak English, or a criminal record. Elderly people, people with responsibilities to care for young children, students, and some occupational groups such as doctors and nurses and clergy are permitted to decline or postpone their service. The ease with which people can be excused from jury duty accounts for the fact that even though over eighty million Americans have been called for service in state and federal courts, fewer than half of those called have ever actually sat on a jury.

After a jury pool of 30–150 people is called, they are each subjected to the *voir dire*, the search for the truth. The questioning is conducted by the judge alone in federal court, and by the judge and both attorneys in state courts. This practice of questioning jurors about their backgrounds and attitudes began during the American Revolution, when everyone was suspicious of everyone else's motives. However, in England, where our jury system originated, questioning of jurors does not occur even today.

During *voir dire*, jurors can be challenged for what is called "cause." This occurs when a potential juror may know one of the parties, or have a financial interest in the outcome of the case. Challenges for causes are unlimited, but attorneys are also permitted to a limited number of "preemptive" challenges.

These refer to attorneys having a chance to challenge someone based solely on a hunch or their own bias.

Lawyers rely on their experience, instinct, and, yes, stereotypes to use their challenges. As you can imagine, I have seen some strange things in my years on the bench. After many trials, I would sit with the two attorneys and politely ask why they had challenged certain prospective jurors. The answers ranged from "a feeling in my gut," "she smiled at me too much," "he didn't smile at me," "the juror would not look me in the eye," and so forth. Most of the time, the reasons made sense.

It is up to each judge to rule on whether the challenges are valid enough to excuse the potential juror. Are the attorneys trying to exclude women, African-Americans, blue-collar people? If it is a challenge that appears to be biased against all African-Americans, or women or Asians or any other demographic group, this is cause for a judge to step in.

Keep in mind that the judge knows a great deal more about the case than the jury might ever hear. The law is strict when it comes to disclosing a defendant's past record, since it does not necessarily prove that they committed the current crime. But judges wield a lot of power and influence over a jury. I know firsthand how hard it is to stay objective.

Before a jury gets picked for a criminal case, the judge has learned a lot about the defendant. In pre-trial hearings, the judge gets to hear about the police and detectives' reports. He gets to learn about the defendant's criminal history. The judge will review a purported confession, if one exists. In these pre-trial hearings, the judge rules on whether or not the jury gets to hear any of this background. The law is fairly clear in not allowing certain information to be seen or heard by the jury. If the police have erred in any way in obtaining the defendant's confession, the judge will probably not allow it to be introduced into evidence. If there is any problem with the chain of custody of evidence, it will probably be excluded. You can begin to see the picture.

Knowing all this puts a heavy burden on any judge who is aware that the jury does not have a clue about these omissions. Trying to stay objective and impartial is mandatory, and after having done this for eighteen years I can tell you that it is very difficult to do, but must be done.

I did have a couple of experiences with jurors who lied just to get on a jury, and then did not adhere to the oath they took. In one instance, I was trying a burglary case that had become a cause célèbre in the system. It involved "Douglas," an African-American man who was a very bad burglar. He was bad because he wasn't very good. He was a "push in" burglar—not the kind that forces his way into your house or apartment when you come to the door, but a burglar who pushes in air conditioners to get inside. He would go to an apartment house or townhouse community, knock on the door of an apartment to make sure no one was home, go around to the side of the house, push the air conditioner through the sleeve it had been installed in into the unit, climb in through the sleeve, and steal whatever would fit into his pockets. This time, the sleeve for the air conditioner had been poorly installed and as Douglas tried to climb in, he got caught by the crotch on a cluster of tenpenny nails. He could not move in any direction without causing severe injuries to his privates.

Eventually the police arrived, and called the fire department to extricate him. The print media then showed up, and since it took hours to remove him, TV was there, too, and there was probably enough time for someone to do an oil painting.

At the preliminary conference, I expected the attorney to ask for leniency, but he surprised me by saying Douglas was a three-time loser and knew he was probably going away for life.

He'd always pleaded guilty, but *this* time he wanted a trial just to see what it was like.

We picked a jury and the ADA submitted over seventy eight-by-ten glossy photos of Douglas stuck halfway into the apartment. I declined to allow the TV footage for the sake of the defendant, who had asked that his torn pants and exposed genitals not be shown. The court officers started a pool as to how quickly the jury might return after I charged them and sent them in to deliberate. Forty-five minutes was the most popular bet, but three full days later, after several notes from the jury telling me they were hopelessly deadlocked, I declared a mistrial. I walked into the jury room to ask the jury if they wished to talk to me about it, because I always considered it a learning experience when jury members wanted to tell me about their experiences on a jury. The foreman was red in the face with anger. He looked at me and the other jurors and reported that an African-American female juror, who had already left the courthouse, had singlehandedly caused the hung jury. The moment she'd walked into the jury room to deliberate, she announced loudly, "I will never vote to convict a 'brother,' no matter what the evidence and the law is!" I reported the juror to the district attorney but they decided not to bring charges against her.

Incidentally, when the defendant was tried a second time, the jury was out just an hour and a half before returning a guilty verdict.

If a jury asked to speak with me after a case was over, I always did, and it usually turned out that they had worked very hard to do the right thing. They would invariably tell me that the most difficult part of their service was trying to understand the law I read to them and how the law I charged them with applied to the case. Many times, juries would send a note to me during deliberations to ask me to charge them again on a particular statute or part of the statute.

I am not a violent person, but have had occasion in my courtroom to clench my gavel until my knuckles turned white, thinking about how much I would love to be able to inflict the same type of pain on the defendant that the defendant had inflicted on the victim. I also knew that the defendant deserved a fair trial under our justice system, and that would bring me back to reality and reason. For example, rape or murder of a child stays with you: in one case the defendant had raped a fourteen-year-old and carved his initials into her chest. Fortunately, in this most difficult case that came before me, the defendant pled guilty and we did not have to go to trial. Presiding over that trial would have been a difficult test for anyone. I know it would have been for me.

The closest I ever came to wanting to cross the line was a case out of Northern Westchester involving three little girls. Both parents worked and they lived a quiet, peaceful, suburban life. They had hired a nanny to stay with their daughters (ages seven, nine, and twelve). An emergency came up for the nanny and she had to leave town for a few days. Meanwhile, the parents had recently met a newcomer at their church who had volunteered to do odd jobs for members of the congregation, since he said he was on disability and had plenty of time. The parents called him, and he agreed to stay with the girls for a day while the agency found a replacement for the nanny.

He wound up tying all three girls up, raping them, and leaving them alone in the house. He was caught and the case was assigned to me. At the initial conference with the ADA and defense counsel, I found out that I had a major problem. The defense attorney did not deny his client's guilt, but said he should be in a psychiatric hospital, not a jail. I actually felt my blood rise and my face flush.

I asked them to wait in the anteroom for a few minutes. I sat in my chair and breathed deeply for a few minutes. I called the attorneys in and asked if they had considered a plea negotiation. The defense attorney said that he had no viable defense other than his client's mental condition. The ADA offered to let him plead guilty to the top count and would agree to my sentencing him to concurrent sentences. It was at this point that I inserted myself in the case by stating that the plea was unacceptable to me, unless the defendant agreed to surgical, not chemical, castration when he was released from prison.

The defense attorney looked at me and said, "You cannot order that, Your Honor!" I said, "I'm not ordering anything. It is up to your client."

He asked for a week to talk to his client. He returned with the ADA the following week, and said his client would only agree to what is called "chemical castration," which in this case involved taking a hormonal drug called Depo-Provera. Depo-Provera significantly reduces libido, and does reduce recidivism rates (i.e., repeat offenses) from 75 percent to below 5 percent for pedophiles. However, the chemical treatment stops working when you stop taking the drug. At that point, recidivism for pedophiles is over 75 percent. I told both attorneys to get ready to go to trial. When the defense attorney asked me what sentence I would agree to, I indicated that if his client plead guilty to all three rapes I would sentence him to seven and a half to fifteen years on each count, to run consecutively. He had already suggested this to his client as a possible outcome and said he knew that his client would agree. This was a narrow escape for me as the judge, because I knew that if the children had to testify, the jury would have seen how cautiously and gently I treated them in the courtroom. They would have taken a message from that.

I remember my friend, Judge J. Emmett Murphy, telling me when I first took the bench, "I give you eighteen years before you burn out." I had no idea at the time how close to the truth that statement was. If not burned out, I was severally burned, with many sleepless nights spent trying to get certain images out of my head. I can never forget the details and images, the torture and the pain of those three girls being brutalized in that quiet house in the suburbs. The absolute terror they must have felt! I still see pictures in my mind that I cannot and will not describe here.

13

Jury Selection: Strategies and Stereotypes

Now I'm going to share with you the real secrets of top trial lawyers in selecting a jury.

Over the years, the legal profession has perpetuated a mostly secret lore about what sorts of people make what sorts of jurors. These classifications of jurors depend heavily on ethnic, class, and racial stereotypes.

Many of the rules of thumb presented in published guides to jury selection are simply adaptations of common stereotypes.

For example: heavy, round-faced people are believed to be more favorable to the defense than slight, underweight, delicate people. Latinos are emotional. Asians are conservative. Jews are sentimental and liberal. Bankers are apt to convict. Women jurors are hard on women defendants.

These superficial stereotypes may be misleading. Maybe, instead of feeling a special bond with a person of his own nationality, an Italian juror might despise an Italian man who is associated with organized crime.

Generally, women are thought to be victim-sensitive; men, more cold-blooded. Salesmen, actors, artists, and writers make good defense jurors, it is believed, because their occupations have exposed them to a wide variety of lifestyles. They are not as easily shocked by crime as people in less adventurous jobs.

Black jurors are generally more sympathetic to defendants and more distrustful of the government than white jurors.

Now you know the basics of selecting a jury: seat-of-the-pants guesswork and instinct.

There is an old joke among lawyers that describes the difference between jury trials in England and jury trials in the United States: "In England the trial begins after the jury is selected. In the United States, the trial is over after the jury is selected."

In 2004, a public opinion poll was released revealing that Americans have a profound belief and trust in the jury system. The poll went on to disprove the popular notion that Americans consider jury duty a burden to be avoided: a majority of those who had actually served on a jury said that they would like to do it again.

In addition, more than 75 percent of those polled said that if they were ever a participant in a trial, they would want a jury, rather than a judge, to decide their case.

Hundreds of people have asked me over the years to help them get out of jury duty. It inevitably leads to my lecturing them.

It is not only an honor to serve, but also an obligation. I tell them that I would not tell them how to get out of jury duty and if they serve on a jury and they dislike the experience, I will buy them lunch.

In all the years, I have only had one friend come back to me for lunch. He'd been selected to serve for a trial that took two months. While he did admit that it was a fascinating experience, he felt it was just too long to serve.

I took him to Burger King.

14

How Much Justice Can You Afford?

Local laws and legal customs varied in the Middle Ages, as they do now. One custom that was fairly common was group responsibility. If someone in a village was convicted of a crime, and if the punishment was a fine, it was assessed against the entire village. How much less crime would we have in local neighborhoods if we brought that practice back!

Other parts of the medieval justice system were unique to the period. The most startling medieval ritual was known as "ordeal of arms" or trial by combat. The two sides fought it out with weapons and the winner was declared in the right. Many medieval chroniclers pointed to the Bible stories of Cain and Abel, or David and Goliath, as justification of the use of God's judgment by combat. For the most part, this was an ancient custom that fortunately died out in medieval times, but I think I'd bring that custom back in limited circumstances. How about public humiliation? Bring back the stock and public flogging. All right, just publish the names of the offenders in the town square—and on Facebook and Twitter.

In Bavaria, up until the ninth century, the defendant had the right to challenge the plaintiff's witnesses. They could accuse the witness of perjury and challenge him to a duel to settle the matter. The case was immediately adjourned until the duel took place, and the duel would often resolve the case if wounds proved fatal. If witnesses lost the duel but survived, they were fined the amount that their testimony would have cost the defendant. (Loser pays court costs! What a great idea!) In France, it was common for litigants to eliminate witnesses by making accusations of wrongdoing against them. This forced the witness to fight and win in order to get his testimony accepted as truthful. To make matters worse, witnesses were allowed champions (someone to fight for them) but only in the case of age or infirmity. Thus, women and children were not allowed to give testimony, for they could not defend themselves if challenged.

Well into the thirteenth century, not only could witnesses be challenged, but the judges as well could be challenged on their decisions. This was the only appeal allowed. Even then, judges tended to be older men, but not fools. I would have liked that appeals process. I would have chosen Arnold Schwarzenegger as my champion.

Dueling persisted into the nineteenth century. With its demise went the ancient custom of trial by combat.

Now we enter the twentieth and twenty-first centuries. The cost of justice is no longer trial by combat, but trial by money; your standing in court depends on who you are. Remember Roman Polanski, charged with having sex with a minor? Zsa Zsa Gabor was charged with assaulting an officer, and Sean Combs was charged with bribery and illegal weapons possession. These are serious charges that would have landed ordinary mortals long terms in jail. But the poster boy for the double standard, Robert Downey Jr., despite his highly publicized busts on drug and weapon charges, has seen his stock in show business soar.

He was even released on several occasions from LA jails to complete movie shoots.

There was nothing wrong with the courts sparing Lindsay Lohan a long prison sentence and determining that the proper punishment for her was yet another attempt at drug rehabilitation. There are thousands of drug offenders that deserve the same compassion, but these drug abusers are not high profile and haven't got the money to hire high-priced counsel to help them. They cannot afford to hire the top legal guns, crack private investigators, and publicists. People with money can level the playing field with the prosecution by hiring these expensive lawyers who give their clients whatever chance at leniency there might be, which would be all right if everyone had the same opportunity.

That's where judges come in, to make sure everyone has the same opportunities. There have been many times that a judge has tread lightly but has had to intervene with a sidebar conference with the attorneys to help an underrepresented offender. It's not a question of bad lawyers, necessarily; public defenders are notoriously understaffed, underfunded, and overworked.

It was always hard to sit on a case when I knew one defendant had an extremely expensive and competent lawyer while the very same charges were brought against a codefendant represented by a competent Legal Aid Society attorney. Sadly, the Legal Aid Society, like most under-funded organizations, does not have the resources to hire the investigators, expert witnesses, and private detectives that a rich person has. It is up to the trial judge to try to level the playing field—no easy task without appearing to the jury that you are taking sides. While it is inappropriate for a judge to inject his or her personal beliefs into a case, judges have an ethical obligation when things are outright unfair to act and to insure equal justice in their courtrooms.

This is not the spin that the media puts on its stories. I have no love lost for the media in general, but I'm begging for a media outlet that strives to tell the truth, unvarnished and straightforward.

I tried the first televised murder case in Westchester County. During a break, I spoke to one of the television producers and asked why they did not ask to televise an ordinary trial, something like burglary or grand larceny, so that the public could get a real sense of what the system is all about. His response was immediate and short. "Judge, if it's not headline-grabbing who would watch it? Our TV audience thrives on sex and violence!" As the old TV news adage goes, "If it bleeds, it leads."

15

Court and TV: "We All Pay the Price"

Over the past few years, the average media consumer would be under the impression that the nation is awash in lawsuits and greedy trial lawyers. Out-of-control juries eagerly punish corporate America with multimillion-dollar penalty verdicts.

We have been told over and over that most lawsuits are frivolous and that the undeserving are reaping the benefits. I cannot recount all the times that clients would come to my office when I was in private practice to see if they could sue for some perceived wrong. The easy answer I always gave them was that anyone can sue anyone for anything.

The real question is: Can you be successful?

Some examples of this phenomenon are:

- In November of 2002, viewers of *60 Minutes* learned that Mississippi was the nation's capital of "jackpot justice," where plaintiffs' lawyers found that juries in impoverished rural areas can be mighty sympathetic toward one of their own going up against a rich multinational corporation. In the story, Morley Safer interviewed Beau Strittman, a local florist who had received a multimillion-dollar settlement in a lawsuit over the anti-obesity drug Redux. The florist alleged that the trial lawyers were bribing jurors to give plaintiffs big awards. "The juries awarded these people this money because they thought that they were going to get a piece of it," Strittman told Safer. Several Mississippi jurors sued CBS for libel over the broadcast. Meanwhile, Strittman retracted his comments about the payoffs saying, "I just said it as a joking statement!"

- In June of 2003, the American Medical Association (AMA) reported in a *Time* magazine cover story that lawsuits were forcing thousands of doctors to leave the profession. "To doctors, the main problems are frivolous lawsuits and multimillion-dollar judgments awarded for tragic but sometimes unavoidable outcomes." Yet only two months later, in August of 2003, a General Accounting Office found that many media reports—and the AMA's claim that malpractice lawsuits were causing doctors to quit the profession because of the malpractice crisis—were false.
- A *Newsweek* story claimed that this country is facing an onslaught of litigation that costs Americans $200 billion annually. But this figure came from a subsequently discredited insurance industry study that included in its definition of *the legal system* overhead and investments, medical bills, lost wages of people who were injured, and insurance industry salaries.

Despite the alarming headlines, American tort lawsuit filings – those that are civil in nature, e.g., negligence, injuries from car accidents – have actually decreased 9 percent since 1992, according to the National Center for State Courts. In Texas, where the population jumped 23 percent between 1990 and 2000, the rate of tort filings fell 30 percent. In California, the rate fell 45 percent. Despite what you might have heard about inflated judgments, a Bureau of Justice statistical analysis found that in 1996, the median damage award was only $27,000.

The skewed coverage of the legal system represents a victory in a sustained twenty-five-year public relations assault on the civil justice system by a highly organized movement funded by the insurance industry, tobacco companies, and pharmaceutical and other corporate giants seeking to limit their liability for wrongdoing. The insurance industry launched the first concerted PR attack in the early 1980s with a series of ads in *Newsweek* and *Time* magazines with the headline "We All Pay the Price," claiming that lawsuits were forcing obstetric gynecologists (OB-GYNs) out of business. If we had lost all those OB-GYNs back in the 1980s, how was anyone born after that?

Then, as now, many of the horror lawsuit stories that turned up in the media proved to be fabrications. You do not tend to read about the false stories reported in the media, because these stories do not sell papers, and they would detract from the impression that the media wants you to have, that they strive to tell the truth.

Only after the recession did the media run stories about finance companies' predatory lending practices, companies that rely heavily on media advertising. News outlets lead with stories about the monetary size of jury verdicts and the portion that might go to the plaintiffs' lawyers. Rather than write about the lack of health insurance that forces sick and injured people to seek compensation in the courts, they write about rural juries that want to bankrupt honest doctors and businesses.

I ask you: How many times do you remember reading a story about a multimillion-dollar verdict being reduced to a much smaller amount by a higher court? No, take a moment and think about it! The media does not like to print such stories. If they did, you wouldn't give the next sensational two-million-dollar broken toe verdict much credibility!

It is practically impossible to count the number of cases that are dismissed because they have no merit. Judges routinely throw out what we deem frivolous lawsuits. Again, these are not the stories you read about in the newspapers or see on TV, because there is no sensationalism, sex, or violence.

I remember when the US Supreme Court ruled that attorneys were allowed to advertise their services. Surprised and saddened, my dad was the first to remark, "That's the end of any dignity for the legal profession."

I agree, and it has only gotten worse. As an attorney who has been a prosecutor, a defense attorney, a civil practitioner, and a judge, I am sickened by the ads you see on television, in the papers, on trains and buses, and in magazines, ads designed to make you feel that they are doing a public service. Do you have asbestos poisoning? Mesothelioma? Have you been in a car accident? Do you have any medical claim, any untreated acne? We will take your case and not take a penny from you unless we get you money!

They leave out the fact that they usually take one-third of whatever they recover for you. Try asking an attorney if he will work on an hourly basis instead of a large percentage. Better yet, offer 15 or 20 percent and see how many attorneys will take your offer!

All too frequently, these "contingency" attorneys counsel their clients that there is always a risk in going to trial, and that they might not recover as much of a settlement as the insurance company is now offering. This tactic results in quick settlements and quick fees for the attorney, and the moment the client approves this tactic, the attorney has failed to earn his fee. If you compare a breakdown of the time he has spent to the fee he is charging, you would be amazed, and this overcharging has been going on for a century or more.

A decade ago, Florida voters approved a ballot initiative limiting lawyer fees in civil lawsuits, and Nevada voters rejected a measure that would have meant penalties for lawyers who bring lawsuits lacking merit. Both measures are ineffective, though, in reducing frivolous litigation. Fee limits reduce lawyers' incentive to bring strong cases as well as weak ones.

The Florida and Nevada measures misjudge the problem: honest lawyers and those lawyers with scruples rarely bring frivolous lawsuits since they have little chance of any settlement. The notion that defendants will settle meritless claims just to avoid the nuisance of litigation is highly exaggerated. Most defendants are repeat players who know that "buying off" weak claims would just inspire lawyers to bring more.

One technique that lawyers have for ending a lawsuit before trial is to bury the other side in paperwork and electronic data. The need for high-priced experts to assist in interpreting specialized evidence can make the high cost of evidence a key reason why trials drag on for months or years—and even then do not always lead to just results.

It is now commonplace for lawyers to hire jury consultants to help the lawyers win on the basis of style rather than substance, precisely because the evidence can be so difficult for a layperson to comprehend.

In fact, the fear of not being understood in the courtroom is a key reason that many companies turn to arbitration and mediation to resolve their disputes. Arbitration and mediation can address issues of both expertise and cost, and alternative dispute resolution is well suited to various kinds of disputes. Certain kinds of cases, such as securities, class actions, and mass torts, are better resolved in the courts. Many juries have told me after trial that they disregarded a lot of the expert witness testimony and just used a common sense approach to reach a verdict.

To reinvigorate this adversarial system, more than mere tweaking is in order. For starters, the dollar amount of recoveries must be limited, and the much-abused discovery rules should be thoroughly reviewed. Judges and jurors need better ways to obtain unbiased education about hard-to-understand evidence.

The use of more specialized courts is another major reform to be considered. Just as there are family courts and surrogates' courts, there should be a great many more specialized courts. There are now drug courts in the criminal justice system—why not specialized courts to handle the types of cases that cause a backlog in our system?

Mine is not a lone voice. There are a lot of judges out there who are as fed up with the way things are as I am. There is little we can do except for throwing out cases that have no merit, while trying to speed the system as much as possible and attempting to do justice at the same time.

This sounds like we are trying to keep several balls in the air at once. Well, we are, and we do it day after day.

So, the next time you are introduced to a judge, give him or her a hug or a pat on the back and tell them how hard their job is and how much you appreciate the work they do. You will be astounded at the reaction you get.

16

THE COURTS AND BIG BUSINESS

DID YOU PAY Enron, Cendant Corporation, or Adelphia Communications Corporation executives? I speak of an entire class of people who should be ashamed of themselves—but are not—and keep laughing at the rest of us. When corporate executives wind up in court, who pays their bills? Sometimes it's the executives themselves, but more often than not it's the shareholders. Other times it's the insurance company, which reluctantly pays the claim under the "errors and omissions" policy and immediately passes the cost on to the consumer by way of higher premiums. Such across-the-board increases make it costlier for honest firms to do business.

Frank P. Quattrone, the former investment banker at Credit Suisse First Boston who was convicted in May of 2004 of obstructing justice, has had his multimillion-dollar legal fees paid by his company throughout two trials. Three members of the Rigas family, who founded Adelphia, have finally settled their case regarding charges that they siphoned off millions of dollars from Adelphia to pay for their family's personal use of a golf course, luxury cars, and, incredibly, their church dues! The company may be out of business now, but the shareholders were still on the hook to pay legal expenses. Adelphia founder John J. Rigas and his sons Timothy and Michael have already received over $24 million from the company and another million from their insurance company. Under the settlement, the Rigas family, after all the fines are paid, will only be left with $25 million dollars, hardly enough to live on. Obviously, I jest!

There is a highly effective and easily implemented solution to the problem of what are called "low-probability" lawsuits. The remedy involves general fee-shifting of the sort found in the United Kingdom. Under that system, if the plaintiff wins, he or she recovers litigation expenses as well as damages. If the defendant wins, the plaintiff reimburses him or her for litigation expenses. If the case settles, the parties can agree on how much to allocate costs.

This system gives judges a chance to identify an unwinnable case, to warn the parties, and thereby avoid the costs of lengthy motions, hearings, and trials. This "loser-pays" rule accomplishes what current reforms are striving for: it discourages plaintiffs' lawyers from bringing claims that have low probability of success. Unlike some current attempts at reform, however, this fee-shifting would work without inhibiting claims that do have a high likelihood of winning. Big business does not like this solution, since it would enable the little guy who has a strong claim, but not the means to bring suit against them. Not surprisingly, the insurance industry and the AMA are also opposed.

Are there other ways to improve the system? How about addressing the incredible backlog of criminal cases crowding the courts?

First, let's follow a typical case from the time the crime is committed to arrest and then entry into the system. A typical case would be a burglary committed by a drug user to get money for his or her habit. There is a witness who sees the defendant enter the house and calls the police. The police arrive and chase and catch the defendant. They ask the witness to come to the police station to give a statement, and they bring the defendant to the station for processing. The defendant is brought before a judge as soon as possible after the paperwork is done, and the judge either sets bail or sends the defendant to jail.

The next steps are what have caused a tremendous backlog of cases. The court sets an adjourned date for the case, and may or may not conduct a preliminary hearing on that date. It depends on the availability of the witness and the police. It depends on the district attorney. Moreover, it *always* depends on how busy the court's calendar is. After a preliminary hearing (a simple hearing in which the DA presents as little evidence as possible), the defendant is probably held for the action of the grand jury. Since there is only one grand jury for the entire county in most jurisdictions, the case can be delayed by several months – and usually is.

A different assistant district attorney presents the case to the grand jury, and if they indict the defendant, the case is then sent to a superior court for motion practice, hearings, and trial. This delay is always many months and by this time, the witnesses have had to repeat their story several times. Motions by the defense attorney and the district attorney can be dragged out and dates have to be set to conduct pretrial hearings (i.e., identification hearings), Miranda hearings if the defendant made statements, etc. If all goes smoothly and the case is ready to go to trial, it *then* has to be sent to the calendar clerk to schedule the trial. The commissioner of jurors is notified how many jurors the judge may need for the trial, and by this time you can see how the system can get hopelessly backed up.

I tell you all this for a reason. When I was sitting on the bench in Westchester and saw how backed up the system was, I thought that if every case in Westchester County was brought to a County Court judge within thirty days of the crime, this expedited procedure would benefit everyone. Defendants would either start their sentences or, in the case of drug offenders, get into a rehab program that much sooner. Witnesses would not suffer as much from natural or induced memory loss. Victims would get a measure of closure in a matter of weeks, not months or years. I went to the administrative judge with my ideas. I suggested that he appoint one judge who would do nothing but conference every felony that occurred in the entire county. The conferences would be broken down to separate days for drugs, violent crimes, property crimes, etc. He listened and looked at me and said, "I suppose you are volunteering for the job?"

With the administrative judge's blessing and an expenditure of only $50,000 for computer peripherals and a second court clerk to schedule over one thousand cases, I was able to conference 1,348 cases by myself in eleven months. The vast majority of offenders either pled guilty, were dismissed, or, in the case of minors, sent to juvenile boot camp. The rest, a small percentage, went to trial. *The New York Times*, which does not usually have anything very nice to say about criminal court judges, wrote an extremely flattering story about me, reporting that I was instrumental in creating and running this program. My principal law clerk, Al Degatano, was entirely responsible for setting up the network between the lower courts and the calendar clerk. He deserves enormous credit for the program's success.

New York State saved millions by not having to try all those cases. They saved an enormous amount of money in not having to jail all those defendants who were immediately placed on probation. Even more money was saved by not having to transport all those defendants back and forth from the jail to the courthouse. Well over one thousand cases never went to the grand jury. Police overtime was cut tremendously, because these cases never went to trial. I could go on, but you get the idea.

Where is that system now? Funny you should ask.

Months after the story was written the administrative judge had a *talk* with me. He explained that now that there was no backlog of cases, he had to assign judges from criminal to civil courts, including transferring some judges to matrimonial court. I probably do not need to tell you how few friends I made among those judges, who detested matrimonial court as much as I did. However, as a result of the transfers, the civil backlog went down since there were more judges to tackle those cases.

The court officers, whom as you know I have great respect for, complained to the administrative judge that because there were so many fewer trials, they were not earning overtime "babysitting" juries when a jury would have to be sent to a motel during jury deliberations (being "sequestered") if they were unable to agree on a verdict during that day's deliberations.

The administrative judge told me that another complaint was this: the District Attorney also said to him, how could the DA argue to the legislature that the DA's office needed more assistant district attorneys because of the backlog workload? That argument had disappeared since the backlog was no longer there.

He failed to mention to me that the Administrative Judge could also not argue to the politicians that he needed more judges since he could not justify the need either.

This is any innovator's dilemma: Is it worth it to try to keep trying to buck the system? "Politics and power and overtime pay" seems to be the overwhelming rule, and to hell with improving the system if it cuts into them. Who cares about the victims getting speedier justice, or the drug addict starting treatment sooner? Well, I did.

My family continued playing a big role in my life. As I mentioned earlier, after my dad died, my mom made every effort to come to court as often as possible. And she *loved* it whenever I was written up in the newspapers. There was a reporter in the courthouse doing background about me for the story about the system I had implemented, and my mom happened to be in court that morning. The reporter got a kick out of Mom and put in a sentence about her at the very end of the story, a remark that she was the only person in the courthouse who could tell *me* what to do. So many people I spoke to in the next few months told me that they had bumped into my mom in Hastings (where she lived) or somewhere else in the county, and that when they said hello she immediately quipped, "Did you know I was written up in the newspapers?" I took no offense at that. It was my mom and I loved her taking over the story. When asked about the story, she would simply say, "Don't you know my son the judge, Peter Leavitt? He was in the story also."

After I retired, I moved to Palm Beach County, Florida, and decided to continue to contribute my time to the court system. I met with the chief administrative judge and he listened very patiently to the strategy I had implemented in New York. I gave him a copy of the statistics, the *New York Times* article, and copies of the forms and paperwork needed to run the system. I told him I would fly Bill Rosvally down to set up the computer programs, which I knew Bill would do. I volunteered to run the program at no charge until it was up and running, until the judges learned how it worked. He asked me for the name and phone number of my old administrative judge.

I question the intelligence of my giving him the phone number of the administrative judge who loved taking the credit for disposing of his county's backlog, but then shut the program down. When I finally heard from the Palm Beach County administrative judge, his response was polite but short. "Judge

Leavitt, it is true that we have a backlog of cases, but the glass is only filled to the brim right now. When it overflows I will call you."

That was eight years ago. I wonder just what my old administrative judge told him.

17

The Judge's Team

It's time for a little soul-searching, some introspection, some plain truths, and some further understanding of how difficult and challenging being a judge is. Obviously, judges are the crux of the judicial branch of our government. They serve the public by using their legal skills and knowledge to impartially interpret and apply our laws. Often they are called upon to serve as neutral referees or fact finders in disputes. Trial court judges must keep hundreds of cases moving through the court system and at the same time ensure that all cases receive full and fair treatment. They preside over cases concerning every aspect of society, from traffic offenses to disputes over the management of professional sports to issues concerning the rights of major corporations to questions about disconnecting life-support equipment connected to terminally ill persons. They decide custody of children, settlement of estates, and on and on. I am sure that each one of you has been impacted in your lives by a judge at some time or another.

All that said, judges cannot be fully effective without the help of a skilled support team. Judges elected in my jurisdiction were allowed to select two people who would work for them, a legal secretary and a principal law clerk. They become employees of the state and are in the court system, but work solely for their judge. I was incredibly lucky to be able to hire Denise Riviezzo as my legal secretary, whom I had worked with when I was an assistant district attorney some seventeen years before. She was terrific. There was nothing she ever overlooked, and everything that I overlooked she would point out to me. She was a very private person but loved to share in my family's life. She was so professional and such a perfectionist when it came to anything that had my signature on it. I was dependent upon her vast store of knowledge when learning the proper protocol for anything to do in and around the courthouse. I also often relied upon her to help extricate me from events I did not want to attend.

You see, judges are asked to go to a lot of events, and some are just not appropriate given the nature of a judge's position. Anything to do with fund-raising is off limits, as are some political activities. Denise was always firm but polite when it came to my schedule. In 1999, my wife Taffy became ill and was diagnosed with cancer. She was undergoing chemotherapy and radiation treatments after she was diagnosed. I was driving her into New York City three times a week and then going to work. The schedule was exhausting and was taking a toll on my health, not to mention what it was doing to Taffy. Because Taffy was getting upset about the burden she was placing on me, without discussing it with me or telling me what she was doing, she and Denise arranged for other drivers to take her into the city for her treatments. Denise reached out and court officers gave up their days off so that I would not have to drive her during the week. I protested until Taffy told me it would make her feel better not having me drive her so often. (It's hard to argue with a compassionate cancer patient.) Denise worked it out.

Denise was the heart and soul of my office. She would gently ask me if I would do a wedding for a friend of hers or some such tiny favor every so often, and usually with abject apologies. I thank you, Denise, for the patience and the love you extended to my family and me.

Then there is the judge's principal law clerk. Without the help of a good law clerk, there is no way a judge could handle the voluminous workload.

Clerks have awesome responsibilities. The principal law clerk serves in many capacities for the judge. He or she may be directed by the judge to hold preliminary settlement conferences with the attorneys. This allows the clerk to discover for the judge the sticking points that might hinder a settlement: who is being stubborn, or worse; who is just plain incompetent.

Choosing the right principal law clerk is a crucial decision for a judge. I had Taffy sit in when I was interviewing law clerks since she was a former copy editor and I felt she would be of immense help in understanding the questions to ask about someone's writing skills. I interviewed many candidates including some "political suggestions" who appeared for the job. Of all the candidates, Taffy really felt that Al Degatano was best able to express the way I thought and spoke. She was right of course, and he was able to do that when working on the drafts of my opinions. Al became my first clerk, and Paula (Al's wife), Taffy, and I became true friends.

Al was a private person. He didn't beat me into work on a daily basis but when he did, it looked as if he had been at work for hours. He was tireless and was a relentless seeker of the law and was always searching for the best way to help his judge. We had many discussions about cases and were sometimes on opposite sides of the result to be reached. We both were willing to listen and learn. Not as easy as you think, because of the enormous workload we had, but when it was one of those "interesting hot potatoes" thrown into my lap, we would spend hours working theories back and forth. We had an amazing respect for each other and truly a remarkable bond.

The judge and his clerk will conference for many hours on some cases and for just a few minutes on others. The clerk will have digested multitudinous briefs and have researched the law so as to present the judge with the essential facts and legal precedents of a particular case. The judge then either writes the decision himself, leaving it up to the clerk to polish, or the judge will direct the clerk to draft the decision. Whichever option the judicial team follows, suffice it to say that these two people become very close. It is essential that the clerk be able to read the judge and interpret the essence of what the judge thinks and feels. This is more than a marriage; it is a solemn bond.

Many judges choose not to make waves. They will just stick to precedent, will not want to take chances, or will fear being reversed; others choose to tilt at windmills. As you know, I am the latter breed. I am proud to tell you that I have been published fourteen times during my career, a record for the district and state that I sat in. To be published means that a judge, recognizing that times have changed and that the law has not kept up, has taken on an established precedent, and that circumstances presented to him give rise to a judicial challenge. A judge may also be published when the facts of a case are so unique that the judge feels it is time for the law to catch up to the present.

A judge may also be published if he writes about the law and it is unique or sufficiently intelligent to be considered worth publishing. I wrote an article that was published in Pace University Law School's *Pace Law Review*. To me that was one of the highlights of my judicial career. It was an article about the law and senior citizens (more on this later).

It is the solemn responsibility of the clerk to protect his or her judge, to know whether or not the judge is willing to fight for what he or she believes in, and to maintain secrecy regarding the outcome of the cases before the decisions are published. In some cases, the amounts of money are so large and the temptations so vast that many judges occasionally have their clerks draft two opposing decisions before the judge himself files the final decision. I was lucky that during all the years I sat, I had two law clerks of the highest caliber that not only served with distinction but also have become lifelong friends. As I mentioned, my first clerk was Al Degatano and the second was Bill Rosvally. I am proud to have known you both and proud of the work you did.

I was in the middle of a very difficult murder trial and decided to take an action that was unique. It was Al Degatano who found the legal authority for me to do it. I decided that the jury had to be taken to the scene of the murder to better understand the testimony they heard in court. A lot of arguing ensued over the field trip when I told all the media people that they would not be allowed to be there. I received all kinds of legal threats, but I told them that they could not take pictures since the jurors would be visible. Only one TV station violated the court's order by parking a block away, setting up their transmitting tower, and taking tape. My sergeant had spotted them and I instructed the remaining court officers to have the jury return to the bus. I took several officers with me and went to their TV truck and confiscated their camera. Their attorneys were at the courthouse before we even got back there ourselves, demanding it be returned. I *did* return it—after the tape and memory had been erased. After the trial, the jurors thanked me for the action I had taken; their anonymity and safety needed protecting and we protected it.

The judge's right arm. The guardian of the robing room. The runner of interference between the judge and the district attorney and all the other attorneys, Legal Aid Society, probation department officers, police officers, and anyone else who wants an unscheduled visit—ladies and gentlemen, I give you the *court clerk*.

The clerk is responsible for making sure that the calendar flows smoothly every day. This is not just scheduling cases to be heard, but juggling extra cases that are inevitably added to the calendar, with dozens of people—attorneys, litigants, and court personnel. The clerk always has cases as standby in case someone calls in sick, a defendant unexpectedly pleads guilty instead of going to trial, or a case is somehow resolved in some other fashion. The clerk has to schedule the judge's conferences, know when to gently interrupt if a lawyer is taking too much time, juggle prisoners from jail who have to appear with the corrections department and court officers, send out voluminous reports every day, and generally do everything else that a judge needs doing during the day. The court clerk gives the judge a daily briefing before each calendar call and warns of possible issues, including possible problems with defendants and even possible problems with attorneys! The clerk is in charge of the jury in the jury room, making sure that they are as comfortable as possible and seeing to their meals. If the jury is sequestered, the clerk and the court officers coordinate their lodging. There are dozens of other jobs that the court clerks do that I have left out, but suffice it to say that it is the clerk of the court who can make life easy or hellish for the attorneys who appear and for the judge who presides. I applaud the good clerks and I know that they do not get the recognition that they deserve.

My court clerk was Lisa, but Lisa was so much more than a clerk. She was also my protector. I cannot remember how many times attorneys and district attorneys would come into the outer office and ask to see me without an appointment. The easy rule I had set up was: if it is an emergency, come anytime; if not, please call Lisa and make an appointment. The rule was violated more than enforced, but if I ever wanted to get my work done, I had to have rules. No one got past Lisa.

She came into my chambers one day just after we had adjourned a murder trial I was conducting. She was red in the face. "What's the matter?" I asked her. She looked at me and said, "Judge, you know that reporter who is in the front row every day?"

I knew who she meant. He represented a nationally known newspaper (which I would name, except that it is hard to fight a libel suit with someone who buys ink by the barrel). I'd noticed that he wasn't here today for testimony he would have undoubtedly found boring—the medical examiner had been on the stand all day.

"Well," she said, "He just called me and asked me to tell him everything that happened in court today!"

Astounded, I asked her what she had told him. She looked at me, gritted her teeth, and said, "I told him *nothing*!" He wound up issuing a story that had nothing to do with the day's testimony, but repeated information he had gathered from the preliminary hearings. Can you see why I dislike the media so much?

With this remarkable and dedicated professional staff behind a judge, the everyday job becomes easier. Other judges, who are not trial judges, have a far different job when it comes to what they have to do on a daily basis, very different from what we who face these challenges every day refer to as, "in the trenches with the blood and guts."

Appellate Court judges—those on the Supreme Court, the appellate courts, and the courts of appeal—do not usually try cases, but review cases based on the trial record from the trial court. These judges spend most of their time hearing oral arguments, researching the law, conferring about cases, and writing opinions. Published opinions from the highest of these courts become the case law for each individual state and serve as legal precedent for subsequent cases. As I mentioned earlier, I have had fourteen opinions published. Some of these opinions have been appealed and have become cited case law, meaning other judges and law school students cite them. It makes me proud to think I was not afraid to take a stance and I became my own brand of innovator while on the bench. I had a great moment recently when my older daughter Karen told me that a friend of hers had just read one of my cases for a Harvard Law School class he was taking.

Judicial decision-making is a structured, analytical process. When deciding a case, judges must consider only the evidence presented—the applicable law and the legal issues presented by the parties. When there is a disagreement about the meaning of the law, judges turn to well-established legal principles to guide their decisions. This principal is known as *stare decisis*—literally, the thing has already been decided—or "the rule of law." In this respect, the role of the judiciary is very different from that of the executive and legislative branches of government. Although it is appropriate for lawmakers to consider the opinions of their constituents when deciding public policy, judges must remain neutral and impartial when deciding cases. The drafters of our Constitution devised these differences to ensure that no individual or group could completely dominate our government. Wise men.

I had a great desire to level the playing field for *everyone.* I referred earlier to a proposed law I wrote that would benefit senior citizens the same way that juveniles are benefited. Most senior citizens' crimes are economic in nature, done to feed or clothe themselves or someone they love (Bernie Madoff's far larger-scale offenses aside). Children get a second chance when they commit a minor crime. They are treated as youthful offenders and have their record sealed. Why not treat seniors who have been law abiding all their lives the same way?

This proposed law was the one that was published in the *Pace Law Review*, but, unfortunately, I could not find a politician or even get the AARP to sponsor it. I guess it's just not politically popular to help people who commit crimes, petty or otherwise. They are simply not a sympathetic group.

I have to go back slightly in my history to tell you about a senior citizen who brought me to the article I wrote years later. When I left the district attorney's office having completed my obligation there, I signed up for the "assigned counsel panel." The panel chooses lawyers who will work for indigent clients for twenty-five dollars an hour. My very first case was an example of why we need a law to protect seniors. But for the kindness and intelligence of Judge James Reap, an injustice would have occurred.

An older woman, widowed, living on her husband's social security, ran out of money before the end of the month. Too proud to go on food stamps or welfare, she went into a supermarket and took a small can of sardines and a roll of bread, and walked out. The big, burly security guard, sensing a major arrest, followed her and collared her as she was opening the sardines. She pleaded with him that she was just hungry, had run out of money for the month, was sorry, and didn't mean to do anything wrong. He ignored her pleas as he handcuffed her and placed her under arrest. She was processed in the White Plains lockup and brought before Judge Reap the next day. Remember, it was my first time ever as a defense attorney.

The clerk, Manny Belmont, called the case and I stood there proudly and announced that my client pleaded not guilty. The judge looked surprised and said, "Both counsel approach the bench!" I had tried numerous murder, rape, and robbery cases, and many other major cases as a district attorney, but I was shocked and worried that I had screwed up my first representation of this poor old lady.

The ADA and I walked up to the bench, and the judge whispered to me, "Counsel, have you never heard of the Jean Valjean defense (from *Les Misérables*)?" I had no idea what he was talking about, but knew better than to argue. He said, "Step back, gentlemen."

I returned to my trembling client, announced that she was going to change her plea, and wished to raise the Jean Valjean defense! The judge looked down and said, "In that case, all the charges are dismissed!" Always know in whose ballpark you are playing. If you want examples of law and grace, look at this judge. No grand speeches, no media, just common sense and justice.

Our government was designed to offer the minority protection from the majority. It is a system of checks and balances not only between the three branches of government, but between the rights of citizens and the government. An independent judiciary, one that operates free from the fear of political retribution for its decisions, preserves this delicate balance.

I get the shivers when I write those words. It sounds so noble. It is. It was the greatest job I ever had. All of the training I had, all the words of wisdom from my brother and dad about the law, all the life advice from my mom, from Pop, the brilliant and quiet voice of Taffy, the little bits of nonconformity from Lonni forcing me to look at another side of the rules and regulations imposed on us—it all made me a better judge.

Taffy was of monumental help to me in all my years of judging. She was always patient and understanding. There would be days when I'd get home, and Taffy would look at me, tell the girls that dinner would be a little later, and suggest we have a glass of wine and talk for a while before dinner. She was wise and compassionate, and I knew she really had feelings for the victims I would talk about. A partner like that is indispensable to a judge.

Judicial independence does not mean that judges are not accountable to the people. Judges are accountable for their actions, not in the sense that they must rule according to public opinion, but by being reviewed by a higher court on appeal. If they act unethically they are subject to disciplinary action, including removal from office, and of course citizens in an election state can vote whether or not to retain or reelect a judge whose term is up.

(Of course, in my case, I was such a brilliant jurist that these questions never came up.)

18

The Roots of Law

Now: on to what's under those robes! Didn't you think when you bought this book that I was going to reveal what we wear (or what we *don't* wear) under those robes? Well, in the summer in a courthouse without air conditioning I would wear shorts. I'm shocked—shocked!—at those of you who had other thoughts!

Seriously though—what is under those robes? The most diverse group of people that you can imagine. I have met hundreds of judges and lectured to more. I have gone to school with them, held conferences with them, and become friends with them. We are sometimes held in high esteem, but, more often these days, held up to public ridicule. If we are attacked in the media, we are not allowed to respond. We are forbidden by the canons of judicial ethics from commenting on any case still pending in the courts, and that includes during all appeals.

When some politician doesn't like the result of a particular case, he or she can call a press conference to denounce the judge. The judge, on the other hand, has no one to defend him. The judge cannot say to the press, "The politician wasn't in the courtroom and didn't hear the testimony." They cannot say that the district attorney failed to prove their case, or that a witness lied on the stand. They cannot remind the public that the law is a strict taskmaster that must be applied evenhandedly even though the public may be clamoring for a different conclusion. Judges are forbidden to discuss any case until there has been a final appeal, which can take years. They cannot say that sympathy has no place in applying the law, and they cannot reason with the press *at all.* They must sit back and endure the slings and arrows until they retire and write a book.

Early in my judicial career, I had a particularly difficult couple of cases in a row where I felt the young people before me deserved a fair shake. I believed these two cases should stand on their individual merits and not on public outrage, and I decided to take a chance on the two boys. Neither case was a violent crime. They were separate thefts from small businesses in economically distressed neighborhoods, and the locals cried out for blood. I gave each of them a chance to start a new path in life.

The press and the District Attorney once again bashed me for being too lenient. When all was said and done, unfortunately one of the boys fell back into a life of petty crime. However, the other young man graduated from high school and then went to a two-year college and has a job in a department store in White Plains, NY. He just needed a chance and perhaps a little bit of guidance.

Although a 50 percent success rate doesn't sound very high it becomes meaningful when you realize you have helped change a terrible path into a good, useful life devoted to giving back to society. Otherwise, these youths are turned over to a system that generally sends these kids back to society worse than before they went in.

No matter how provocative and compelling a case may be, no matter how pure the motive, the constitutional protections of the individual's rights for even the most heinous and unsympathetic person cannot be ignored or set aside in the name of the greater good. As I've relayed to you several times, no matter how unpopular a decision, it is the job of the judge to dispense justice, not to bend to the intimidations of political pressure or popular opinion. For this the judge is abused, maligned, and criticized, and rarely applauded. The reward is in the ability to look into the mirror each morning and smile at yourself. The joy is in knowing that you have done justice.

My sister Lonni was particularly angry for the way that I was being attacked in the media, and holding her temper was not one of the things my sister was usually successful at. She wanted to be able to speak to the media in my defense, and it took a lot to convince her that she was not allowed to. So instead, she vowed to work to change the rules for judges. Such a pal! If there was something unfair put in front of her, rest assured she would take up the cause.

There are judges that are content with the status quo, but I want to tell you about someone who was bold enough to take a stand and change everything: Hammurabi.

This remarkable king and lawgiver, who reigned from 1795–1750 BC, represents one of the earliest examples of a ruler proclaiming publicly to his people an entire body of laws, arranged in orderly groups so that a man could read them and know what was expected of him.

The code was carved on an eight-foot-tall black stone monument that was intended to be viewed in public and was rediscovered in a city in the Persian mountains in 1901. Let us then take a brief look at parts of a code written over 3,700 years ago. Hammurabi was far ahead of his time not only in his foresight but also in his sense of justice and fairness, and he has had a profound influence on the way I think about and practice law.

The code regulates, in clear and definite strokes, the organization of society. It regulates trade and commerce, both foreign and domestic. It sets forth the law on family and marriage.

A judge who blunders in a law case is to be expelled from his judgeship forever, and heavily fined. The witness who testifies falsely is to be slain. If a builder constructs a house badly and it falls and kills the owner, the builder is to be slain. Talk about a warranty! If the house also kills the owner's son, the builder's son is slain. You can see where the Hebrews learned their law of "an eye for an eye."

These grim retaliatory punishments take no note of excuses or explanations, but only of the facts—with one striking exception. An accused person was allowed to cast himself into the Euphrates. Apparently the art of swimming was unknown, so if the current bore him to shore he was innocent, and if he drowned he was guilty. Now *this* is speedy justice with no appeal! Is this an example of Hammurabi's influence on me? I always wanted to slay builders who built houses that collapsed.

Hammurabi was equally clear regarding matrimonial law. The code, sounding suspiciously like today's prenuptial agreements, allowed a proviso to be inserted into the marriage contract, that a wife should not be seized for her husband's prenuptial debts, and likewise, that a husband was not responsible for his wife's prenuptial debts, and, in any case, that both together were responsible for all debts contracted after marriage. A man might make his wife a settlement by deed of gift, which gave her a life interest in part of his property, and he might reserve to her the right to bequeath it to a favorite child, but in no case could she leave it to her family.

How simple, how fair, how uncomplicated divorce court could be today!

Others of Hammurabi's matrimonial laws were not quite as reasonable, to say the least. If she had been a bad wife, the code allowed him to send her away, while he kept the children and her dowry, or he could degrade her to the position of a slave in his own house, where she would have little more than food and clothing. She might bring an action against him for cruelty and neglect and—if she proved her case—obtain a judicial separation, taking her dowry with her.

No other punishment fell on the man. If she were proved to be a really bad wife, however, she was drowned. If she were left without maintenance during her husband's involuntary absence (an early form of the draft?), she could cohabit with another man, but must return to her husband if he came back, the children of the second union remaining with their own father. Willful desertion by, or exile of, the husband dissolved the marriage, and if he came back after he had deserted, he had no claim on her property and quite possibly not on his own, either.

In Hammurabi's criminal laws, the ruling principal was the *lex talionis*: an eye for an eye, tooth for a tooth, limb for a limb was the penalty for assault upon a freeman, the cutting off of the hand that struck a father, the loss of an eye for prying into forbidden secrets, the loss of a surgeon's hand that caused loss of life or limb. No such thing as medical malpractice insurance! This symbolic retaliation as punishment of the offending member was a cornerstone of the Code of Hammurabi.

The death penalty was freely imposed for theft and other crimes coming under that heading, including entrance into the temple or the temple treasury, illegal purchase of or from a slave, selling or receiving stolen goods, common theft in the open market, kidnapping, fraudulent sale of drink, or placing someone in danger of death. The manner of death is sometimes specified: gibbeting (hanging by chains and left to rot) for burglary, for getting a slave's brand obliterated, or for procuring a husband's death. Burning was the choice of execution for incest with your own mother, entering the vestal sanctuary, theft at a fire, adultery, rape of a betrothed maiden, bigamy, seduction of a daughter-in-law, or bad conduct as a wife. In rereading the Code of Hammurabi, I wondered what it would have been like in my courtroom to have been able to emulate the queen in *Alice in Wonderland* and shout, "Off with his head! Off with his head!"

Not having the ability to sentence miscreants according to the Code Of Hammurabi, judges have to ad lib every so often. This is true when sometimes you push a judge a little too far. There was a judge in my own courthouse who had an IBM executive before him for sentencing on a driving-while-intoxicated offense. It was his first offense, and usually the judge would be lenient but firm, but the IBMer's attitude was smug and outright rude.

The judge, having finally lost his patience, looked down at him and in his most stentorian voice said, "I will now pronounce sentence on you. Since you seem to have no remorse for what you have done, I direct that you be taken from here to a scaffold located outside the courthouse and that you be hung by the neck until you are dead!" The IBMer fainted.

When the terrified defendant awoke, the judge informed him he'd just wanted to teach him a lesson and reduced the sentence to a license suspension, a fine, and an admonishment. This is an absolutely true, documented sentence handed down by a Westchester County judge.

The more I think about it, the more I believe that there is a great deal to be said for judges retaining their sense of humor.

Do not get me wrong: I loved my job, but when I arrived home after a particularly rough day, there were these little smiling faces greeting me, expecting me to behave normally, to be able to play a little before dinner, and to be a normal father and husband. Sometimes it was hard, especially if I'd had a particularly stressful day.

But I was very lucky. I had a thirty-year love affair with my wife and two girls who knew when it was time to take a ride with me on my riding lawnmower or to keep me company in my workshop. They also knew when Dad needed a little time alone before dinner. I wonder about all the other judges who were not as lucky as I was. I do not think that everyone is cut out to be a judge. I think you need to have a lot of training in dealing with people in extreme circumstances and never lose your sense of humor or your humanity.

Even though I worked for ten years as a fireman and another ten years as an Emergency Medical Technician in and out of emergency rooms, being a judge was by far the most stressful job I've had- it involved tremendous sacrifices, and provided huge rewards.

They ought to do a study about post-traumatic stress syndrome in judges. If I survive writing this book, I think that'll be my next project.

19

Threats: "I Still Look Behind Me"

So far I have touched on my family, food, the Brooklyn DA's office, local courts, judges making law, juries and grand juries, jury nullification, trial lawyers, the media, rape, trial by combat (my personal favorite), celebrity justice, judges, law clerks, legal secretaries, and court officers.

I keep telling you how much I loved my job and felt that every day I went to work, a new challenge would present itself to me. Unfortunately there were those days that were not so good.

I remember a chilling moment one day when I returned to my chambers and court officer Major Bobby Kane was waiting for me. He asked to come into my chambers and closed the door behind him. I was surprised and worried. Is everything all right? Is anyone hurt or injured? It seems they had received a letter, and when it was screened they knew that they had to take action immediately.

Our courthouse was named after Judge Richard Daronco who was shot to death by the father of a divorcee for whom he had been the judge in the case. The father did not like Judge Daronco's settlement terms and expressed his displeasure by killing him. The letter sent to me at the courthouse vilified me, referring to a case that had taken place years ago. The last page of the letter stated, "The only way to get justice is to kill the judge." Major Kane suggested I go home immediately and assured me that the police would be waiting at the house to protect my family. My security team escorted me to my car after checking to make sure no one had planted a bomb underneath it and I followed a county police car to my home. Shortly after I arrived home Major Kane called to say that they had the letter writer in custody.

The New York State police sent an expert who arrived at my home within the week and conducted a security survey to make my home safer. I cannot tell you the details of what they did for safety reasons, but I felt a lot safer when they finished.

I still have that letter and a photo of the sender. I advised the local authorities about him anytime I moved, which was the best I could do, I guess. I take a lot of precautions, as my security people advised me to do. I still hold a full-carry gun permit, having received police training from a very patient sergeant in Mount Vernon. I also went for training in hand-to-hand personal combat from an Israeli who was a former member of the Israeli Army and learned to drive in a defensive driving course a police instructor taught me.

I am convinced that there are a lot of crazies out there. I do still look behind me when I am driving and in crowds and if you doubt that it is something that you would continue to do if you were I, you have never had someone threaten to kill you.

20

Witnesses: Being "Too Credible"

Enough about all the fun we have as judges. Let's look at some of the problems we face when confronting witness testimony. I served as the key witness in a murder case while I was on the bench, but before we discuss the circumstances surrounding the only sitting County Court judge to be a witness in a murder trial in New York State, perhaps a look at the nature of witness testimony is in order.

Examining witness testimony I hope will make you a better observer of court cases you see in TV shows and movies. You might gain a little insight into how wrong the media is when they say, "The prosecution has *only* a circumstantial case against the defendant." The reliability—or lack thereof—of eyewitness testimony is a perfect segue to my personal experience.

Do you recognize the names Victoria Price or Ruby Bates? They were the key witnesses in the infamous 1931 Alabama trial of the Scottsboro Boys.

In those days, a lot of people would ride the rails to look for work, or just ride the rails as a way to pass the time until they had to spend another homeless night on the street. One night, twenty to twenty-five men and women were riding a freight car when a fight broke out between some white and black hoboes. The conductor called ahead and a "gang of citizens" met the train at its next stop. The whites immediately jumped off the train, but the black boys, nine of them altogether, were arrested.

There were two white prostitutes hiding in the same freight car, Victoria Price and Ruby Bates. In order to avoid prosecution for vagrancy and a violation of the Mann Act, which made it a federal crime to cross state lines for "immoral" purposes, Victoria and Ruby claimed they had been raped by nine young black men, one of whom was twelve years old. In Alabama at that time, trials took place within days of the arrest, and they were frequently quick and nightmarish. All but one of the black boys was sentenced to death. Ruby later recanted her story, however, and medical testimony eventually showed that the rapes had never occurred. The case was tried again, and this time the defendants were represented by New York attorney Samuel Leibowitz, who was later elected a Supreme Court judge in New York and came to be known as "Hanging Sam." The prosecution challenged every prospective black juror and was successful in seating an all-white jury.

The case was going badly for the prosecution and in his summation, one of the prosecutors asked, "(Is) justice in this case...going to be bought and sold with Jew money from New York?" Leibowitz immediately made a motion for a mistrial, which was denied. The jury came back into the courtroom, and announced that the decision to find all nine men guilty took five minutes.

When Sam Leibowitz returned to New York and was interviewed he said, "If you ever saw these creatures, (referring to the jury) these bigots whose mouths are slits in their faces, whose eyes popped out at you like frogs, whose chins dripped tobacco juice, whiskered and filthy, you would not ask how they could do it!" How I wish I could turn a phrase like that!

Judge James Horton, who had tried the cases, spoke in private to one of the doctors who had examined both Ruby and Victoria. He told the judge that there were no signs of rape, bruising, fresh semen, or any other trace of forced entry. Judge Horton then made the announcement to a stunned courtroom that he was setting aside the verdict and ordering a new trial. Judge Horton was never reelected again.

The story of the Scottsboro Boys is one of the most shameful examples of injustice in our nation's history. The results of these trials were unthinkable. Evil can come in the guise of otherwise normal people who, for reasons of selfishness, careers, ideology, or a desire for society's approval, are indifferent to the consequences of their acts. Due to the career-minded prosecutors and the self-serving, groundless, wrongful accusations of two women, nine black teenagers had their lives ruined. This wasn't simply a matter of bad or incorrect testimony, just plain perjury. So can we really be sure of the veracity of "eyewitness" testimony, even from a so-called victim?

It is a sad comment to make, but Caucasians make terrible witnesses when it comes to identifying Asians or African-Americans, and the reverse is also true. In over thirty years of trial experience I have observed, all too often, witnesses who have made mistakes in their identification.

When we hear about circumstantial cases, we think *weak case*. Let's take a somewhat closer look.

Let's say you have just bought a new snow blower, used it once to clear your driveway, and then stored it in an outdoor shed. It snows overnight and you are looking forward to using your new toy again. You go to the shed and see the door is partly open! Sure enough, the snow blower is missing. You look around and see clear footprints in the snow leading up to the shed and tire tracks leading away. It has snowed, as I said, so the trail is clear. You follow them to your neighbor's garage, peek into the window, and see your new snow blower partly hidden under a tarp. Any eyewitness to the crime? No. Any witness at all? No. A circumstantial case? Yes. A strong case? Absolutely!

Often scientific evidence, although not direct evidence, is the clincher in a case. You'll remember that earlier I pointed out the DNA rape case that had shaky identification, but solid scientific evidence that proved that the defendant was guilty. So, when you read or hear the media trying to hype your interest by shouting, "But the prosecution only has a circumstantial case," take a step back and see what the case is really all about. See, it is no fun for the media to report on a slam-dunk, since that would not spark your interest.

While I am sure that someone out there in our vast world of reporting honestly tries to report the facts as they really are, I am convinced that their editors have to spike that story, tell them to jazz it up, or to simply save the punch line for the eleven o'clock news. I just despise their unwillingness to tell a straight story. Journalism has been sacrificed for sensationalism.

All right, no more teasers. I will get to the time I testified in a murder case in the very courthouse in which I worked.

I was a sitting judge in Westchester County Court and an Acting New York State Supreme Court justice, trying all those terrible cases you read about. I was also a certified EMT with the Chappaqua Volunteer Ambulance Corps. Now, The vast majority of the calls we would get in Chappaqua were for slip and falls, heart attacks, car accidents, and the other usual small-town stuff. As you are aware, the Clintons live there, and it is kind of a sleepy, nonviolent, gang-free community, with no major drug problems and rare assaults and personal crimes. So, when my pager went off one evening, I was in the kitchen as I recall, and the voice from my pager reported "multiple GSWs."

I had to think for a moment before I realized it meant *gunshot wounds.*

I raced out of the house, pulling my EMT jacket on as I left. I went to the "barn" where we kept the ambulance. Our driver, my friend Andy, was already there, and he and I and a second EMT, Dan, raced to the scene. When we arrived, it was bedlam. I have a great deal of respect for the police. They do a job I would never want. These local police had lost control of the scene. They were allowing family members to move through the crime scene. They did not safeguard the evidence. The victim's mother was screaming in anguish and running back and forth between the two victims. Her husband was one of them and her daughter the other. Her daughter was a young woman, two and a half months pregnant, lying on her back in the driveway, with blood running from a wound in her head. She had another wound in her chest and, grotesquely, there was an empty shell casing from an automatic pistol sitting on her sternum. There was an older male victim sitting propped up against the house who seemed to have multiple gunshots to his upper left chest area. I assessed the young woman and knew immediately that she was dead.

Dan called to me to help him with the man. I called to Andy to call Pleasantville Ambulance Corps to back us up, and he told me they were already on the way. Meanwhile, the young woman's mother was still running back and forth in the crime scene, screaming, "Save my daughter! Save my husband!" and the police were just standing there waiting for us to tell them what to do. I saw Pleasantville EMTs arrive and whispered to one of them that she was gone, but to take over treatment immediately and asked them to treat her gently since her mother was there watching. I put a pressure bandage on the man's wounds, and Dan and the police assisted getting him onto a stretcher and into our ambulance.

This is now the part that generated all the notoriety in the court case later on. If you are the police, and if you have a victim who is still alive but not speaking yet, a victim who has been shot by an unknown person, wouldn't you stay with him? Of course you would. But the officer decided not to do that, following us in his patrol car instead. Say what? Not what Dan and I were worried about; we had a patient to care for. Dan and I shouted at Andy, to drive "Stat!," which I know you know means *as fast as possible.* I called Northern Westchester Hospital and luckily there was a staff meeting there that evening, so when we arrived, doctors, anesthesiologists, surgeons, nurses, and X-ray technicians would be there ready to meet us. We were less than five minutes away from the hospital. As fate would have it, our victim came to when we were three minutes out and pushed the oxygen mask away from his face. Dan gently replaced it and tried to calm him: "It's ok. We are almost at the hospital. Just breathe easily." I was holding a pressure bandage on his chest and was very close to him. He calmed down for a moment, but then pushed the mask away again, looked straight at me and said, "I'm done. I'm finished. Rukaj killed me. Rukaj did it!" Then he again lost consciousness, and, despite heroic efforts at the hospital, never regained it.

I now had this problem: I was sure that Dan had not heard everything that the victim had whispered to me, and I knew from my legal background that this victim had just made what is called a *dying declaration.* I also knew that this statement would be admissible in a court of law. The policeman was the one who *should* have heard his statement, but he wasn't there. I had just become the only person who could identify the killer.

I was interviewed that night by detectives and subsequently by the district attorney's office. They informed me that I would have to testify at trial. They had found the killer, who turned out to be a former boyfriend of the female victim—he had shot her in a jealous rage and then shot her father-in-law, who had come downstairs to try to save her. When the ADA came to my chambers many months later and told me I was going to be called as a witness that afternoon, I was a little apprehensive. I had spent my career listening to countless witnesses (civilian, police, and scientific), but now I was to be the witness. I went to the judges' lunchroom for some solace and advice, and after a few moments, the Honorable Kenneth Lange, who was trying the case, came in laughing. He was laughing so hard that he had trouble stopping. We insisted that he tell us what in the world was so funny. When he regained his composure he sat down and looked straight at me.

He told us that the defendant's lawyer had asked the judge to exclude me as a witness and not allow me to testify. We all looked at Judge Lange and asked what his legal rationale was. Judge Lange hesitated, chuckled, and said, "He said that Judge Leavitt is *too credible*!" The laughter in that room was relentless. I finally got to ask him how he had ruled on the objection and he said, "I granted it in part, you cannot tell the jury what you do for a living during the day!"

That broke the tension for me. I took the stand, testified as I have just related it to you, and the defendant's attorney cross-examined me for less than two minutes. I am convinced that he did not want to tangle with me, knowing who I was. I admit I was a bit nervous on the stand, but I was there for such a short time and I knew the procedure so intimately that it was not difficult or traumatic. I will confess that we laughed for many years at the motion to exclude my testimony, but by now you know I have no problem laughing at myself or being the butt of the humor.

Being able to laugh at yourself is an important lesson I learned from my mom. Let me try to paint *that* picture for you.

I was very young and filled with wonder at the life I had at the time. My parents had rented a vacation home for the summer on Lake Oscawana in Upstate New York. We were having a great time swimming and fishing and making new friends, my brother, sister, and I. My mom, as usual, had company staying with us that she constantly had to cook and clean for, but this time it was *good* company—my grandparents Minnie and Pop. It was always a joy for me to be with them. Pop was always teaching me how to build something or fix something. My dad would stay in the city to work during the week and come to the house for the weekends.

At the time of this story, it was a Saturday; all seven of us had just finished another of my mom's really good dinners. I remember the meal since the trauma that took place that evening makes everything stick in my mind: summer salad and potato latkes with applesauce. My mom considered this an appropriately light meal since it had been so hot that day. My sister went to bed early as usual, and Mom was in the kitchen with Minnie, cleaning up. Dik and I went outside to play and made the now infamous mistake of leaving the screen door open too long. A small fruit bat flew into the kitchen and the screaming began. Pop and Dik and Dad and I came running in to the kitchen to see what the problem was. The poor little bat could not find his way out. Pop grabbed a broom to swat it. Minnie got a can of insect repellent. Dad grabbed a pot of hot water from the stove, and Dik got a softball bat, I was holding the screen door open and everyone was swinging and spraying and running in circles in the tiny kitchen. Just as the bat flew over my mom's shoulder, dad threw the hot water at it, catching Mom full on. Pop went to swat it and hit Mom in the back with the broom. Minnie sprayed insect repellent in her face and Dik, barely avoiding hitting her in the head with the softball bat, still hit her in the behind. I still had the door open and shortly after that, the bat calmly flew out and we spent considerable time ministering to my mom. We washed the bug spray out of her eyes, toweled up the water (it wasn't too hot, thank God), made sure the broom and baseball bat injuries were minor, and then just burst out laughing. Oh, how we laughed! You know how when you laugh really hard, tears come to your eyes? We laughed that hard. From then on my mom was the one who insisted that we tell that story to everyone who would listen, just to give them a laugh. You have to be able to laugh at yourself she always said, I agree.

She was able to prove that point again when we took her to her favorite restaurant to celebrate her ninetieth birthday. She rose to say a few words after all the toasts and speeches were over. She quietly looked out and, still able to make people laugh and poke a little fun at herself, she said, "Thank you all for all the gifts. I have to say I'm not sure I invited all of you here today, but thanks for coming!"

You have to love a lady like that.

21

Addictions: "Five Manhattans for Lunch and Nothing to Eat!"

Professionals entrusted with our well-being are the last people you might suspect of drug addiction, and yet they are as likely as anyone else to abuse alcohol and other drugs. Many doctors, lawyers, and other licensed professionals suffer from alcohol and chemical dependencies and studies show that licensed professionals have the highest incidence of depression of any occupation. As many as one-fourth of surveyed professionals exhibit symptoms of clinical depression, which is more than twice the incidence in the general population. The American Bar Association has estimated that nearly one-fifth of all US lawyers suffer from alcohol or substance abuse, more than three times the incidence of the general public.

It's no surprise that some doctors look to drugs for support. Taxing responsibilities, intense patient relationships, exhausting hours, and easy access to drugs are a potent mix. There is also what is called, "MDeity syndrome," an attitude among some doctors of omnipotence, power, and uniqueness.

My, my! That certainly sounds like many judges I have known. What's that, a chink in the armor? You betcha! Judges are not sacrosanct. They are susceptible to all the usual ills and problems that beset everyone else. Perhaps because of their perceived lofty status, a great deal of their transgressions are either ignored or covered up, much like those of police, celebrities, professional athletes, and politicians. (Let's see. Is there any group I have not offended yet?) There have been innumerable times that a court officer has had to suggest to a judge that he recess for the afternoon because he appeared too drunk to proceed with court. Of course, this is done at sidebar where no one can hear, and the smarter judges take the advice.

When I was an assistant district attorney in Westchester, Taffy wanted to watch me prosecute a murder case. She came for the morning session and the judge who was presiding, dismissed the jury for lunch, and since he knew who my wife was, looked at her and said, "Young lady, will you be so kind as to join me for lunch?" Startled but flattered, she agreed, and when they returned to court for the afternoon session, she gave me the most quizzical look.

We proceeded with testimony, but at around three o'clock the sergeant announced that we were going to adjourn for the day. The judge looked up and excused the jury with the usual warnings not to discuss the case, and stepped down off the bench with the help of the officer. When everyone had left the courtroom, my wife came over and said, "The judge had five Manhattans for lunch and nothing to eat!" I liked that judge, but only if you appeared before him in the morning.

Once most professionals are in recovery, they can move forward with their careers. Requirements vary, but most states allow judges, physicians, lawyers, pilots, nurses, and others in an approved recovery program to remain licensed. These programs allow for retention of personnel and training assets, provide a vicarious learning process to other individuals who may want to seek help for alcohol and drug problems, and have demonstrated enormous success rates for long-term recovery.

Earlier, I mentioned that our government has at times sought to legislate our moral behavior. What an enormous waste of time, energy, lives and money. In looking at addiction, we are dealing with an individual's right to treat his or her body as they see fit. The sad lesson we have learned is that no matter what penalties are attached to the use of alcohol and drugs, they are going to be used and abused.

If you ask anyone in the DEA (Drug Enforcement Administration) if we are making progress in stopping drugs coming into the country, they will tell you off the record that it is worse than ever. The prison population is well over 50 percent drug related one way or another. If we are to do anything to stop the criminals making the fortunes they do in drug trafficking, the government is going to have to wake up. There are outraged people out there who cannot reconcile that drugs should be legalized, under any circumstances, for any reason. Then there are people who have studied the situation and lived in it, and know that there has to be a change. There are also many law enforcement groups that have websites in favor of legalization. A trend has started around this country with more and more states legalizing medical marijuana.

If I were to become this country's benevolent dictator, I would plow the tobacco fields under and plant marijuana, legalize all drugs, and have government-run centers to dispense them. I would create a program that controls who gets what and how much. The drugs would be clean and many of our farmers who are struggling to keep their farms productive could grow poppies or marijuana and be able to feed their families and stay in business instead of what is happening to them now. I could go on for hours but you get the idea. Is this extreme? Probably. Many judges feel that our system has failed in this respect. We have had to send countless people to jail instead of to rehabilitation.

The justice system cannot solve the problem if it continues to address substance abuse as if it were a crime rather than a public health issue. More than $4 billion is spent annually on border control efforts, construction of new prisons, and law enforcement, only to fill prisons with sick people who remain untreated. The most effective countermeasure to the addiction epidemic is to encourage, sometimes even coerce, individuals into treatment. Of course, starting with education at an early age will go a long way toward preventing this scourge.

The American Bar Association (ABA) has been working diligently to integrate substance abuse and addiction treatment into the judicial system. The ABA supports the unified family court movement, which combines all the essential elements of traditional family and juvenile courts into one entity and contains other resources, such as social services, that are critical to the resolution of a family's problems. Substance abuse treatment is very often of more importance in cases heard before the unified family courts than any other single issue.

Under a reformed system, where drug-related criminal offenses are concerned, a defendant might be given the opportunity to choose a family drug court rather than a normal trial. This type of court is currently in existence in about twenty jurisdictions in ten states. They offer substance abusers intensive drug treatment, as well as a range of support services for family members.

I have personally endured watching the nightmare of losing a loved one to alcoholism: my brother Dik. Could it have been prevented? I don't know, but I hope we will teach our kids in our homes and in our schools more about addiction. I hope, too, that we will have early intervention strategies in place when we identify a problem. I hope that parents and teachers will be trained to spot symptoms, and to realize that to act is better than to remain silent and hope that someone else will do something. I hope that professionals will act, rather than turning a blind eye, when they see a colleague who needs help. I hope that this happens in police stations, doctors' and dentists' offices, in the Bar Association, in the courts, and in the halls of Congress.

I continue to hope. I wish I had been able to do a lot more a lot earlier to help my brother. I do not know if it would have helped, but I think it might have made a difference. The family tried for years, but an addiction is all consuming. Even though Dik had gone to AA and was dry for years before he died, the alcohol had so destroyed his system that he was unable to survive the heart attack he suffered at age 48, and we all felt a sense of guilt for not doing more.

22

Children and Crime: "Hi, Judge. You Did Me a Favor. Thank You."

When I start to think about children, I think back over the years to the times I prosecuted them, judged them, counseled them, sent some to prison and some to boot camp. It has become clear that children's crimes are getting more violent. This complex and troubling issue needs to be carefully understood by all of us, including parents, teachers, and, especially youth officers and judges.

Children as young as four or five can exhibit violent behavior – beyond normal roughhousing, that is. Parents and other adults who witness the behavior may be concerned, but the general feeling is a hope that they will grow out of it. Violent behavior in a child at any age, however, always needs to be taken seriously. Violent acts in children can include a wide range of behaviors: explosive temper tantrums, physical aggression, threats or attempts to hurt others (including homicidal thoughts), use of weapons, cruelty toward animals, fire setting, intentional destruction of property, and vandalism.

Whenever parents, grandparents, teachers, or any other adults become concerned about a child, they should immediately arrange for a comprehensive evaluation by a qualified mental health professional. Early treatment can help. Treatment generally focuses on helping the child to learn how to control his or her anger, how to express anger or frustration in appropriate ways, how to be responsible for his or her actions, and how to accept consequences.

There were so many teenage offenders that I had to deal with as a Town Judge and so many more as a County Court judge, that I thought that I had seen almost everything that kids could do to strangers, one another, and to themselves.

As I said before, I was assigned many of the most volatile and difficult cases by the administrative judge, but you'll get no complaints from me. I loved all the attention these cases got, and how they motivated the attorneys to conduct extensive legal research before they began.

It was May of 1998 when one of my more intense youth violence cases came before me. I went to the courthouse as usual and my legal secretary Denise Riviezzo greeted me as she did every morning, but she had that *look* on her face. She followed me into my chambers and said, "You've caught another hot potato, Judge!" and I knew that I'd been assigned another high-profile case.

It involved a fifteen-year-old high school student at Roosevelt High School in Yonkers, who attacked her social studies teacher with a hammer. The teacher was Dawn Jawrower and she was pregnant with her first child at the time. The girl was Jalise Salvatto and she was accused of smashing Dawn several times in the head and body with the hammer. Jalise was indicted for second-degree attempted murder and first-degree assault.

At the arraignment before me, the prosecutor stated that, but for the heroic acts of the other students that day, he believed that the teacher would have been killed. He also indicated that Jalise represented a very high risk of flight, and that she was being treated as an adult—which is permissible regardless of age when a crime is considered serious enough. Nevertheless, the ADA asked for only $100,000 bail. I promptly set it at $500,000, commenting, "I am looking at what appears to be...a hateful, vicious, mindless act of violence."

Phil Reisman of *The Citizen Register* wrote about the case before the trial. His September 29, 1998, column stated, "It is a miracle that Dawn Jawrower is alive today and preparing to give birth. She suffered two skull fractures as a result of the April 7th attack, for which there is no rational explanation. Who can explain such an angry, brutal act?" His remarks echoed the feeling of everyone in the courtroom. Why? How did a fifteen-year-old get so angry with her teacher that she tried to kill her?

I have been involved in thousands of cases in my career as prosecutor, defense attorney, and judge. I served in the army, and I've witnessed things that a lot of people only read about. As a volunteer fireman, I've treated burn victims and carried dead pets out of house fires to their grieving owners. I saw more tragedy and pain during the ten years I was with the ambulance corps than you'd find in three dramatic TV shows put together, but still I cannot fathom this fifteen-year-old's actions.

Dawn Jawrower stood five foot three inches tall. She cared about her students and she contacted Jalise Salvatto's parents to inform them that their daughter was failing her class. Jalise had been cutting classes, missing tests, and not completing her homework assignments. Dawn hoped that they might be able to help, but her effort to help resulted only in Jalise Salvatto's brutal attack.

The attack was sudden and vicious. Jalise went to school with the hammer and went to Dawn's classroom. She knocked on the door and when Dawn answered, Jalise did not utter a word, just struck Dawn in the head and knocked her back into the classroom. The student hit her teacher in the head a second time, then in the neck, then the shoulder. Several students ran to Dawn's aid and probably saved her life. One student kneeled at Dawn's feet after the attack, repeating, "I tried to stop her. I tried to stop her!"

Dawn suffered two compressed skull fractures, underwent three hours of surgery, and had to have titanium rods placed in her head. She made a full recovery, thankfully, and gave birth to a healthy baby boy, Nicholas John, six months after the attack. She had the full support of the school community, but received attention she'd have been willing to do without. She was interviewed on *The Maury Povich Show* and, as Phil Reisman reported, she received letters of encouragement from around the world. And although she laughs when she admits it, she was even mentioned on *The Howard Stern Show*.

There was an awful lot of pretrial maneuvering on the part of both the defense counsel and the DA. District Attorney Jeanine Pirro is quoted in the press as having stated, "I will not agree to a plea bargain that involves anything less than the maximum sentence of ten years in prison. This is not *Let's Make a Deal*." Once I was assigned the case, the defense started a letter-writing campaign seeking leniency from me prior to trial. This is improper and I refused to read the letters, turning them over to the defendant's attorney, who denied starting the campaign.

The next bit of legal maneuvering involved the defense's announcement that they were going to introduce psychiatric evidence to defend Salvatto. This caused another delay when the ADA insisted that they have the opportunity to have *their* psychiatrist examine Salvatto. I granted the adjournment but told both sides to be prepared to hold pre-trial proceedings and the trial immediately thereafter.

While we waited to go to trial, the District Attorney's office relented and withdrew the charge of attempted murder, either through a sense of compassion or a feeling that they could not prove the elements of attempted murder. (After their psychiatrist examined Jalise, they would have had to reduce the charges anyway.) Jalise Salvatto then pleaded guilty to assault in the first degree.

Now I was free to read the letters and the probation report to try to understand this girl's reasoning and some explanation for her actions. The letters from the Salvatto family and friends and members of their church all pleaded for compassion, without giving me any information about Jalise that was relevant. The probation report strongly recommended that she receive psychiatric counseling.

On March 17, 1999, I spoke to Dawn Jawrower and saw the horrible red scars on her head, which she had learned to hide well with her hair when out in public. She had returned to teaching, but at a different school. She remained mostly calm but a bit nervous before sentencing. When it came her turn to speak, she was brief. "I want Jalise to get the help she needs to realize she has a lot of potential," she said. "All I ask of the court is that the sentence she gets is for her benefit." She added that she relived the incident almost every time she looked at her infant son and realized how close he had come to never being born.

Jalise Salvatto spoke at the sentencing and apologized to her teacher. She said she hoped that Dawn could forgive her someday. "I had a lot of counseling this past year to help me understand why I exploded like that. I know you always looked out for me and wanted the best for me and I'm sorry."

As you can imagine, how Jalise should be sentenced was not an easy decision for me. This victim, a schoolteacher who only wanted to help, was compassionate and forgiving and suffered a nightmare that she would have to live with for the rest of her life. A fifteen-year-old troubled girl who had no thought of the consequences of her acts now faced prison and the need for a great deal of help. Where are the guidelines for a judge in a case like this? How does one decide what is right and fair when you cannot understand the act itself?

On my desk in my chambers sat a small brass plaque with the engraved motto "*Homo sum humani, nil a me alienum puto*": *I am a man and nothing human is strange to me*. I thought about this quote a great deal and did what I thought was right in the sentencing, notwithstanding the outside pressures put upon me. I had to dig deep into my conscience and my background to decide upon this sentence.

All of the personal history that I have shared with you greatly influenced my decision.

Just before I sentenced her, I asked Jalise why she had carried out the attack. Her answer to me was, "I don't know." I sentenced her to a term in state prison for the maximum period of time—two and a half to seven years, with six months of mandatory counseling while there. I felt that Jalise was not going to change without a radical move out of the environment she lived in. She wasn't attending school regularly, not listening to any parental advice, and was heading into more trouble according to the Probation Department report that I read. I advised Jalise that if she were to change her ways, and obtain her GED (high school equivalency) diploma while in jail and go to counseling, that I would recommend minimum time for her to serve.

Research studies have shown that much of youth violence can be decreased or even prevented if the risk factors are reduced or eliminated. Most importantly, efforts should be directed at dramatically decreasing the exposure of children and adolescents to violence in the home, community, and through the media.

On that note, I am so upset every time I hear about yet another school shooting. I was sure that something would be done after the shootings at Columbine High School in Littleton, Colorado, and especially after the terrible attack on Sandy Hook Elementary School in Newtown, Connecticut. I think Columbine may be more infuriating to me since the authorities knew about Eric Harris before the shootings took place. In 1996, 18-year-old Harris, together with his friend, 17-year-old Dylan Klebold, had created a website which contained violent video game images and material on how to make explosives. Harris had been diagnosed with mental problems and was put on a prescription anti-depressant. In 1997, the mother of a Columbine student, Brooks Brown, saw the web site and was so disturbed by it that she filed numerous complaints with the Jefferson County Sheriff's office. She believed Harris was dangerous because his web site contained death threats directed against her son.

When the investigator accessed the site, he discovered numerous death threats, not just against Brown but also against several other students and teachers at Columbine High School. Harris also wrote about his hatred of society, his gun count, that he had made pipe bombs and his desire to kill those who annoyed him. Investigator Michael Guerra wrote a draft affidavit requesting a search warrant of the Harris household. He NEVER filed it. The affidavit was concealed by the Sheriff's office until 2001. There have been Grand Jury investigations into the cover-up but it makes no difference, the authorities knew about Harris and did not act.

On April 20, 1999, Harris and Klebold went to Columbine High School, planted a bomb and then proceeded to fire multiple weapons at students and teachers. They fired shotguns and handguns a total of one hundred and eighty eight times, killing 12 students and one teacher and wounding 21 others – including Brooks Brown – before turning the guns on themselves. They were armed with two shotguns, two pistols and ninety-nine explosives. It was the deadliest mass murder on a school campus in the United States since 1927.

Now, we have to turn to Sandy Hook. Just the name causes me to become angry that nothing has changed since this tragedy. Adam Lanza, the 20-year-old shooter, was another mentally disturbed young man who had an obsession with violence and had easy access to guns in his home. Lanza had been diagnosed with Asperger's syndrome (a milder form of autism), sensory-integration disorder and obsessive-compulsive disorder, and was prescribed an anti-depressant drug. After four psychiatric sessions, his mother objected to his going to a psychiatrist and he stopped going to treatment and stopped taking the medication. He had been a student at Sandy Hook for a short time when he was younger and that seems to be the only connection he had with the school (there have been conflicting reports stating that his mother had volunteered at the school years earlier). It was also reported that he played violent video games. His mother was a gun enthusiast and kept several guns in her home, and would often take her son to a shooting range, ostensibly to teach him how to shoot. A former teacher of Lanza's related that he seemed to be obsessed with destruction and war.

On December 14, 2012, Lanza shot his way through a glass panel into Sandy Hook Elementary school and murdered twenty children and six adult staff members. Before he started this rampage, he had murdered his mother at home, shooting her in the head four times. This became the deadliest shooting at a high school or grade school in US history.

Very little has changed since this monstrous act. It was not until January of 2013 that New York State (the first state to act) enacted the Secure Ammunition and Firearms Enforcement Act. In April of 2013, Connecticut and Maryland both enacted new restrictions to their existing gun laws. Ten other states went the opposite direction and enacted legislation *loosening* their gun laws.

Are there any answers? Is there a simple or even a complex way to stop this butchery? We are a violent country, a nation founded through a Revolution and which was almost torn apart by a deadly Civil War. We get into sometimes-fatal fights during road rage. We fight over parking spaces and sales at department stores. We create violent movies and video games and many parents place few restrictions on the media their children watch and interact with. We see problems in children and try to fix them with a pill. Is it educating the parents, the teachers, the entire community to identify and intervene when they see a child in trouble? Yes, but that's only part of the solution.

After witnessing forty years of violence in cases I've tried and presided over, as well as through my personal life experiences, I do not have the answer. Would I like to have no guns used outside the home except for hunting for food? Yes. I do not believe the 2nd Amendment of the Constitution should have been perverted through the efforts of the NRA (National Rifle Association) to change the right to "a well regulated militia..." to "You can bring your guns to Starbucks." Should each state pass stricter regulations? Should there at least be background checks everywhere, including gun shows? Should every child who has acted violently be screened by a psychiatrist? I truly wish that I had any answer to this nightmare we live with, which does not seem to be getting any better, but these may be some of the answers.

In the realm of youth violence, judges have an awesome responsibility. So often we are faced with the situation of having to decide if a teenager should be severely punished for their wrongdoing or not. When dealing with a nonviolent crime, judges have a wide range of choices: a stern lecture and a clean record, probation with conditions that fit the child, boot camp, or, finally, if it is deemed necessary, jail.

Whenever I decided in my mind to give a youth a chance and sentence him or her to probation, I gave them the "fire and brimstone" speech I'd designed to scare the heck out of them. I would go into the ramifications of what I would do to them if they violated the conditions of the probation I was imposing on them, and how lucky they were that they weren't being sent to jail. I would peer down with my most serious face, and I could tell if I was getting through to them.

One particular day, I had a young boy standing before me who had committed his first offense. He was represented by Rebecca Schenk, a Legal Aid Society attorney whom I admired and respected for her intelligence and fervor in representing her clients. She had convinced me to take a chance on her client. As I was going through my usual terrifying speech, I realized that this kid was smirking and barely paying attention to me. I glanced at Rebecca, who had seen the same thing, and who raised her eyebrows and gave a small shoulder shrug. Just then, my court officers brought in a prisoner who was scheduled for the next case on that day's calendar and sat him against the sidewall of the courtroom.

This jailbird was an old customer. We'll call him "Paul." The month was October and Paul had committed a trespass into a scrap dealer's yard so that he could spend the winter in jail rather than out on the street. As they say, "Three hots and a cot ain't bad for the winter."

Paul was one of the more unattractive people I have ever seen. He had horrible acne all over his face, very little hair, and what hair there was had become matted and unkempt. He had two visible teeth, one on the top and one on the bottom, and they did not match up. He sported a huge belly that he was never able to cover with any shirt and a badly healed broken nose. He was plug ugly!

He was listening to me try to lecture the smirking boy, and seemed to sense that I was getting nowhere. I raised my voice a bit, looked at the young boy, and said, "Look at me! If you violate the rules I have set down for you, I will send you to jail and I will make sure that Moondog (I made that up as I pointed to Paul) is your cellmate!" Paul, picking up on the moment, opened his mouth, showed his two teeth, and grinned ghoulishly at the boy. A brief moment later, Rebecca asked if she could have a short recess before I finished sentencing her client. It was an unusual request, but I trusted her judgment and granted her a few minutes to step outside. When she returned to the courtroom she asked to approach the bench. When she and the district attorney were close, she whispered to me, "I think you got through to him, Judge. He just wet his pants!"

Sometimes you have to make it up as you go along.

I never saw that young man in my courtroom again. I did see him late one afternoon at the Galleria Mall in White Plains, however, working part time after school at a store there. He looked at me and said, "Hi, Judge. You did me a favor. Thank you." That was enough reward for a long time for me.

23

Anatomy of a Trial

Thus far, I've gone in-depth about many of the more significant and colorful cases that have come before me. Now I'd like to tell you about the most high-profile case of my judicial career, known as the "Dobbs Ferry Deli murder." From the incident through the arrest, jury selection, trial, sentencing, and appeals, there were a number of firsts I'd never experienced. I hope to give you an insight into what happens behind the scenes in a high-profile case, as well as what you'd ordinarily not learn from the media.

During jury selection, prospective jurors' cars had been keyed, they had to walk through a gauntlet of demonstrators, and much more that I had never had to deal with before. This was not the usual well-mannered courthouse or courtroom that I was used to. I was a fairly new judge in White Plains when the case was assigned to me, on the bench for only three years. Considering all the high-profile cases that I tried during my term, I have always wondered if the administrative judge loved me or hated me. I know that the selection of a trial judge is supposed to be random with names pulled out of a drum, but I remember my dad telling me, "There is no such thing as coincidence if it keeps happening."

It was on October 3, 1996, around 5:15 p.m. in Dobbs Ferry, NY when Charles Campbell drove into the parking lot of the Venice Deli located at 225 Ashford Avenue, and parked his shiny black Corvette in a spot that had been marked "Reserved for Patrons." The owner of the deli was an Italian-American named Richard B. DiGuglielmo (who will henceforth be referred to as "DiGuglielmo," and his son as "Richard D.," for clarification). DiGuglielmo saw Campbell parking his car in front of his store and rushed out to confront the motorist. Charles Campbell was an African-American. DiGuglielmo had had more than twenty-eight prior incidents with non-patrons parking in his lot, and he had been accused of shouting racial, ethnic, and sexist slurs at anyone who parked in front of his store. Some of the complainants who called the police said that they had been pushed, sworn at, slapped, choked, and punched. Many of them had filed complaints against him, but the Dobbs Ferry Police Department never prosecuted any of them. Several of the complainants also asserted that the police tried to discourage them as much as possible, mentioning that DiGuglielmo's son was a cop in New York City.

Witnesses testified that DiGuglielmo told Campbell not to park there if he wasn't a customer. Campbell told him he was going across the street to get a slice of pizza and would come back to the deli to buy a soda.

Campbell walked across the street to the pizzeria and when he looked back across the street, DiGuglielmo was putting a no parking sticker on the passenger side of the Corvette. Campbell went to confront DiGuglielmo and a fight broke out.

It is unclear from the witnesses who threw the first punch, but as the fight started, DiGuglielmo's son-in-law Robert Errico joined the fight against Campbell and then Richard D.

DiGuglielmo, DiGuglielmo's son, joined in. This threesome beat Campbell so badly that DiGuglielmo broke his hand punching him and then broke Campbell's cell phone by hitting Campbell in the head with it. Campbell struggled to his feet and ran to the trunk of his car and retrieved an aluminum baseball bat. Witnesses stated that DiGuglielmo and Errico continued to advance at Campbell, who struck at DiGuglielmo and Errico's legs with the bat. Richard D. went back into the store to get his father's .32-caliber pistol. Most of the witnesses reported that Campbell then backed away when Richard D. emerged from the deli, moving toward Campbell.

Richard D. shot Campbell three times without any warning. The wounds were fatal. Death and tragedy, all of it caused by the anger of the deli owner over a parking space.

This was truly a senseless death. There were accusations in the press that DiGuglielmo had hurled racial slurs at Campbell. There was a tremendous amount of pretrial publicity and all three men were indicted by a grand jury, DiGuglielmo and Robert Errico on charges of second-degree assault and Richard D. on two counts of murder in the second degree and second-degree assault.

The protests started almost immediately since Richard D. was an off-duty New York City policeman at the time of the shooting. There was speculation that because he was "on the job," he had the prior twenty-eight complaints against his father swept under the carpet. The statements from some of these complainants seemed to corroborate this.

There were protesters gathered at the deli sometimes two hundred strong. The Reverend Al Sharpton joined them at least one time. As the press reported, Jeanine Pirro was accused by the defense lawyers of inflaming racial tensions by issuing statements that at least one witness had heard DiGuglielmo say to Campbell: "You fucking nigger, you can't leave your car here!" This was substantiated in an eight-page document filed by the prosecution, detailing the witnesses who heard him cursing at Campbell and providing their statements.

The district attorney presented the case to the grand jury and the case was set down for motions, hearings, and trial.

When there is a long delay before a trial—when attorneys make their motions and judges rule on them and after all the hearings are held—there is usually a lull in the outside activity. Not in this case. The protests and demonstrations never stopped and the media became a hungry wolf for any tidbit of information about the case. Then the big guns arrived.

Reverend Sharpton appeared again, this time at the courthouse, with fifty followers to conduct a prayer vigil in support of the victim and his family. This by itself would have been harmless had I not received an anonymous call that morning threatening my life if a "dead black man doesn't get justice." My security people never found out who the caller was. I also received threats from the other side of the case with a call that warned me to be careful to do "what was right," since the caller "knew" that I was anti-Italian. (As an aside, even though I do not have to justify or dignify that kind of stupidity, as you know, my chosen principal law clerk and legal secretary were Al Degatano and Denise Riviezzo. Enough said.)

There were several pretrial motions and many decisions that I had to make. Richard D. had hired defense lawyer David L. Lewis, who had gained prominence with his vigorous defense of *Fatal Attraction* killer Carolyn Warmus. Lewis again accused Jeanine Pirro of inflaming passions by using the "race card" in her discussions with the media.

I had decided to conduct the trial immediately following the hearings. I also decided all the motions, including motions to issue a gag order for the prosecution, to preclude certain testimony, and other technical motions. In reality, as I have mentioned before, the jury may never get to hear all there is to hear about a defendant's or victim's background if the judge rules that either is improper testimony. For instance, if DiGuglielmo did not take the stand, all of the accusations by those other motorists about his vicious temper and racial bias could not be introduced at trial (and they were not).

After the hearings were completed, I called for the attorneys to meet in my robing room so that I could set out the rules for jury selection and the trial. (The robing room, unlike my more comfortable and spacious *chambers*, is a small room just behind the courtroom containing a small desk, chairs, and a coat rack for the judge's robe.) I wanted to make sure that the trial did not become a circus and that the attorneys understood that I would not tolerate any grandstanding. There were five lawyers in the room: three for the defense and two assistant district attorneys. My principal law clerk was there, as was a court reporter who was setting up her machine. Suddenly, there was a knock on the door and my sergeant said that he was sorry to interrupt, but that the Reverend Al Sharpton wanted to meet with me before the trial began. I looked at the sergeant and calmly said, "Tell the Reverend I cannot meet with him. Absolutely not!"

The sergeant hesitated, smiled at me, and closed the door. When he left, both the prosecution and defense attorneys applauded and told me what a smart decision that was, and said that whatever might have been said at such a meeting would not be accurately reported to or by the media. I had no doubt in my mind that it would have been just as improper for me to speak with Reverend Sharpton before the trial as it would have been for me to speak to the DiGuglielmo's local parish priest from Dobbs Ferry, had *he* asked.

It was at this meeting that David Lewis, the defense attorney, and I had our first confrontation. I informed all the attorneys that after I extensively questioned each juror, they would each be allowed twenty minutes to question each group of fourteen prospective jurors. David Lewis started arguing that he needed twenty minutes for *each individual* juror and the other attorneys chimed in, agreeing. I quietly informed them that the law allowed me to severely limit the time I allot for *voir dire* and if they kept arguing I would further limit all the attorneys to considerably less time; the law in the state of New York allows a judge to set such a restriction. This was not done for a petty display but to let them know who was in charge. After this small clash, all the attorneys understood that I was the one in control of the courtroom and that this was not going to be a Hollywood-type trial.

The next step was to select a jury.

We all knew it would be hard to find potential jurors who had not read about the case, seen the protestors outside the courthouse, or formed an opinion about it. Jury selection went smoother than I thought it would since I stopped the attorneys from making comments that had nothing to do with the *voir dire*, when they were just trying to make speeches. I would stop the proceedings, bring all counsel to sidebar immediately, warn them about the rules I had set down, and state that any further violations of my rules would be dealt with summarily and harshly. Control of the courtroom is essential to any high-profile case. That is why I mentioned the O. J. Simpson case earlier, because I believe that Judge Ito did not adequately control that trial.

The prosecutor on the Dobbs Ferry murder trials was one of the best trial attorneys that ever appeared before me, Assistant District Attorney Patricia Murphy. When she appeared before me on any trial, I knew that I had talent in the room. Believe me, judges want good attorneys in their courtroom. I have had the unfortunate experience of having bad lawyers who will object to every question the other side asks just because they think it makes them look good to the jury, but it is much easier to have lawyers who are fully prepared and who know the rules than inexperienced or incompetent ones.

Whenever ADA Murphy picked a jury she used a trick that not only impressed the prospective jurors, but everyone else in the courtroom, including me. Typically, I would have the court clerk select fourteen prospective jurors from the more than 100 sitting in the courtroom and seat them in the jury box (fourteen being the capacity of the box). A clipboard with the fourteen names of the jurors would be handed to the defense attorney to use to question each juror, and then the prosecutor would be handed the board. In this case, all three defense attorneys questioned the panel and then ADA Murphy was handed the clipboard.

The usual procedure used by almost all attorneys was to hold the board and look down to find a name of a prospective juror and then ask, "Mr. Smith, can you promise me that you can be fair and impartial to my client in this case?" and a myriad of other questions. However, when ADA Murphy was handed the board that day, she did what I'd always seen her do when picking a jury: she glanced at the board and put it down on the prosecutor's table. She would then approach the jury box and ask the first of many questions, such as, "Can you promise me that if the prosecution proves its case to you beyond a reasonable doubt, that you will have no hesitation in finding the defendants guilty?" Then, without looking or hesitating she would start at the number one prospective juror and ask, "Can you, Mr. Smith?" After he answered she would move on to number two and ask, "Can you, Mrs. Cameron?" and then would proceed all the way to the number seven juror in the first row, using everyone's name from memory. She would then hesitate, and everyone thought that she would have to go and look at the board again, but after a few seconds' pause she went to number eight and continued through all fourteen prospective jurors, having memorized all fourteen names in mere seconds, very impressive to anyone who watched her. I believe ADA Murphy's trick was to listen carefully when the other attorneys were questioning the jurors and pay careful attention to the names. Glancing at the clipboard was merely misdirection. Sorry to give that away, Ms. Murphy, it still looked remarkable.

After the jury was selected, I decided to have five alternates seated since I knew this was going to be a long and difficult trial, and I thought that I might have to replace a juror if someone fell ill or needed to be excused for another reason. The jury consisted of five men and seven women. One of the women was the sole black juror on the panel.

The media coverage was so onerous to the jury that they sent me a note complaining about the paparazzi, so I made special arrangements for the jurors to enter the courthouse through a secure entrance, keeping the photographers from taking pictures of them and parking their cars in a secure area and be escorted to that area at the end of each day in court.

Every time I entered the courtroom, it was packed with supporters from both sides. There were the media people in the front two rows and, almost as if it was staged, the entire left side of the courtroom behind the prosecutors' table was a sea of black faces with a corresponding sea of white faces on the right side behind the defense team. There was also a very large contingent of court officers present throughout the trial.

Opening statements were delivered and there was no mention of race playing a factor in the case. The prosecution led off with two eyewitnesses who testified that Charles Campbell was protecting himself and was backing away when Richard D. shot and killed him. A nurse who witnessed the shooting testified that she rushed over to Mr. Campbell to try to help him and that DiGuglielmo ordered her to "just get out of here—you didn't see anything!" and he refused to let her help him. She went on to describe the look on Richard D.'s face: "I would say he looked enraged." She also testified, contrary to the other witnesses, that she thought that Campbell swung the bat at DiGuglielmo's head and shoulders but the prior and subsequent witnesses said Campbell only swung at their legs.

There were many more witnesses who testified, including three young boys who were riding their bikes near the scene—one of them was behind Campbell when Richard D. fired the gun, and you could feel the tension in the courtroom when the boys testified, since it was just plain luck that he wasn't hit by a bullet. All three boys reinforced the prosecution's position that Mr. Campbell was backing away when he was fatally shot. The defense claimed that it was self-defense but had no credible witnesses to back up their claim.

The prosecution put forty civilian and police witnesses on the stand, including the medical examiner.

The highly charged atmosphere of the courtroom gave way to an angry exchange of words between the two sides during one witness's testimony, and for the first and only time in my career as a judge I had to really raise my voice to call for quiet. I had the court officers lock the doors and keep everyone in their seats while I sent the jury out. I called a meeting of all the attorneys at sidebar. I instructed the attorneys to speak to their respective spectators and warn them that I would have them forcibly removed if there were any further outbursts. First, I addressed the entire courtroom and told them that I would treat them with the respect I expected from them and that I was aware of how emotionally hard it must be for them to listen to this testimony. David Lewis then addressed the spectators sitting on his side of the courtroom. Pace University Law Professor Randolph Scott-McLaughlin, who was the legal adviser to the Campbell family, addressed the other side of the courtroom.

The prosecution finished presenting its case and ADA Patricia Murphy announced, "The people rest, Your Honor." It was an incredibly emotional moment and I called a recess to let everyone catch their breath.

The defense called several witnesses but the most important one was the defendant himself, Richard D. He testified that he was protecting his father and that it was self-defense. He denied the prosecution's claim that he used racial slurs and denied that he told a nurse at the hospital that he was glad he did it.

The defense called an orthopedic surgeon to counter the prosecution's testimony that DiGuglielmo broke his hand beating Mr. Campbell, testifying that the injury could have come from a blunt instrument like the baseball bat Campbell was holding. They also called character witnesses to the stand. In light of all the prior witnesses who testified, it appeared that there were no defense witnesses that were able to clearly substantiate the self-defense claim. Neither DiGuglielmo nor Errico took the stand. Forty-eight witnesses in total testified in the trial.

Many of the prosecution's witnesses testified that Campbell retreated at least fifty feet from his attackers and was not swinging the bat when he was shot. The defense contended that Campbell was three and a half feet away and was swinging the bat at DiGuglielmo.

The testimony of all the witnesses put into question the distances between DiGuglielmo, Richard D., Errico, and Charles Campbell. I believed that a trip to the scene of the incident was necessary for the jury to really understand and be able to visualize what had taken place. This was the trip that I talked about earlier, when I confiscated the TV camera because it was being used to tape members of the jury.

I sent the jury to the jury room, addressed the spectators and warned them about not following us. Then I spoke directly to the media. I told them that they were not allowed to follow us to the scene or be present. There were a lot of statements made to me about free press and this is a free country and they could go wherever they wanted to and more such arguments. I then quoted the law, which states wherever the judge goes, so goes his courtroom. In other words, wherever I am, I set the rules when I am conducting court business. The news people scrambled to leave the courtroom; I am sure they were headed to call their respective lawyers to see if I was right.

I believe that although it was a very unusual step to take and it took a lot of security to bring the jurors to the scene, it proved to be very worthwhile, since after the trial some of the jury members stated that it was helpful for them to be able to really visualize the distances they had been hearing about.

On October 22, 1997, one year and nineteen days from the time Charles Campbell was killed, both sides addressed the jury with their closing arguments. As I listened, I realized why David Lewis was regarded as an exceptionally talented attorney. He was clear and concise and pointed the jury toward the victim's conduct, contending that Mr. Campbell threw the first punch. He stated, "At every stage of the confrontation, it was Charles Campbell who advanced it."

ADA Murphy delivered what I consider to be the finest closing of her career. She responded to Lewis's oratory by reviewing the witnesses' testimony and said at one point, "There is no excuse, there is no mitigation, there is no justification for how these three men treated another human being, Charles Campbell."

The next day I spent more than two hours instructing the jurors on the law pertaining to the case. The most difficult part of the instructions was the portion on *justification* (self-defense). As I discussed earlier concerning the Hopeton Minott case, this is a difficult statute to easily explain to a jury. I looked at the faces of the jurors and knew that this portion of my charge was in fact the hardest part for the jury to understand. Since judges are not allowed to stray from the exact words of the statute, I felt powerless to try to further clarify the definitions. When I had finished the charge, I instructed them to return to the jury room and begin deliberations. They worked the first day for over five and a half hours. I excused the alternate jurors and had them escorted to their cars to avoid the demonstrators and the paparazzi that were waiting in the parking garage to try to talk to them. None of the alternates responded to the media's questions.

After this very long day of jury charge and deliberations, I made the decision to send the jury to a motel for the night. I always felt badly whenever I had to sequester a jury. There are a lot of instructions to give them. Do not talk about the case, do not watch television reports about the case or read any newspapers, there will be supervised calls, and on and on. Especially in a high-profile case such as this, the court officers had to be extremely vigilant since I had excused the alternates and no one wanted to have to try this case a second time.

We resumed the next day and the speculations began. Courthouse legend says that if a jury comes back very quickly, the verdict is usually guilty. If the jury stays out a long time, it will usually be not guilty or some compromise verdict. In my experience I believe that neither generality is really true. I also believe that juries in the great percentage of cases do the right thing. I waited all day in my chambers and would only return to the courtroom if the jury had sent out a note to have me read part of the charge back to them or if they wanted to hear some of the testimony read back. Whenever that happened, the courtroom would fill up again with all the spectators and all the media. It was a long, long day and you could feel the tensions rising in the courtroom. I sent the jury to the motel again at the end of the day.

Friday was a repeat of Thursday except that everyone in the courthouse was sure the jury would reach a verdict and not want to deliberate over the weekend. They were wrong. The jury worked until late in the day and once again I sent them to the motel for the night.

Everyone returned to the courthouse on Saturday but this time the feeling was different. The courthouse was empty except for this case. The hallways echoed with footsteps and the elevators were quiet with so little traffic. I waited in my chambers again.

When the court clerk notified me that the jury had sent a note out for me and that she thought that they might have reached a verdict, I immediately went down to my courtroom. They had deliberated all morning and we were all very anxious to have a conclusion to this very disturbing case.

When I arrived in my robing room, I put on my robe, and when the court officers had security in place and all the spectators and media were in place, I entered the courtroom. I had the court clerk hand me the envelope, had it marked as a court's exhibit, opened it, and read aloud its contents: "We the jury have reached a unanimous verdict on all of the charges." I was about to have the jury brought in to deliver the verdict when my sergeant approached the bench and asked me to please call a brief recess to talk to me on an urgent matter. Surprised but nonetheless completely trusting his judgment, I announced that we would be taking a brief recess before the verdict was announced. There was an audible sigh from the assembled as I walked off the bench.

The sergeant accompanied me into the robing room, followed by the court clerk and my principal law clerk. He asked to please speak to me alone. Of course I agreed and, considering the ongoing threats I had received from both the black and the Italian communities, was immediately nervous about what he was about to tell me.

I asked him to take a seat and he looked at me and quietly said, "Judge, I need at least an hour before you take the verdict." I looked at him, astounded, as I had never had this type of request in any trial or proceeding I had conducted. I asked him why and he responded, "I have to contact the Dobbs Ferry police to cordon off the Venice Deli [where the shooting took place], since our intelligence people have learned that if there is an acquittal there may be trouble at the scene of the murder. I have to contact the Westchester County police to make sure that the busloads of demonstrators that may be notified to come to White Plains are kept under control. I have to contact the White Plains police to cordon off the courthouse and they will be bringing their riot control units. I have to contact the New Castle police to station a car at your house. I have to call in twenty court officers to guard the courtroom and this floor." I looked at him and asked how credible the threats were and he said that he would not be employing this much manpower if they were not credible. There are things in life that I would have preferred not to hear about. When I asked him if there was anything else, he went to the door and called an officer into the room.

"Judge," the sergeant said, "You know Mike, one of our court officers; he will be with you for extra security and if anything happens, please do exactly what he tells you." The sergeant looked at Mike, a really big guy, and said, "Mike, thirty-six."

I had no idea what that meant but I knew better than to question the wisdom of my sergeant. We walked out of the room and I told my court clerk that I would be in my chambers for at least an hour. She did not question why. Mike walked with me, and as we stopped unexpectedly, he said, "Judge, I want to show you the safe room in case anything happens. I will take you from the courtroom and lock you in, and you are to please wait until we come to get you." At this point I can only recall that I wanted to get to a phone as quickly as possible to talk to my wife and warn her about the situation. He took me to a small storage room and I hoped that I would never have to be locked up in it.

We went to the secure judges' elevator and Mike entered with me. This by itself was highly unusual since court officers did not generally use the judges' elevator. We got to the seventeenth floor and Mike walked down the long corridor to my chambers. I said, "Excuse me, Mike, but I have to go to the men's room." Mike had me wait by the door and he entered and checked it out and then said, "I will be here when you come out." When I came out, Mike followed me into my chambers, and that's when I learned that "Mike, thirty-six" meant that his orders were to never be more than thirty-six inches away from me.

What went through my mind during that waiting period was anxiety for the safety of my family because it is rare that a case becomes personal for a judge. I was not as concerned about my safety for some reason. It is true that judges get blamed for almost everything they do, sentences they hand down, divorces they grant, support payments they award, estates they have to rule on, but rarely does it become so dangerous sounding and so in your face. Having been faced with these kinds of tough decisions before, I knew that no matter what happened in the courtroom, I would have no problem doing justice. My fear was the danger to my family.

I spoke to Taffy, explained why there was a police car parked in our driveway, told her to stay in the house for the time being, and tried to reassure her that I did not think that there would be any trouble. I then spent a very restless hour and a half waiting to hear from the sergeant. I asked Mike just how serious he thought the situation was and all he said was, "Judge, follow me please." We walked down a very long corridor to the windows that faced the Galleria shopping mall across the street from the courthouse. He told me about the security briefing that all the court officers went to every morning concerning this case. Looking down from the 17th floor window, Mike pointed out a black vehicle, a big bus and about a dozen police officers wearing SWAT uniforms standing outside the vehicle. They were carrying heavy weapons. I went back to my chambers and waited. I did not ask Mike any more questions. For some reason or other, I do not think that I really wanted to see those sights since it was now clear to me that the threats were very, very real.

When the call finally came from the sergeant I was quite a nervous person. Mike and I went down to the robing room and as I entered the sergeant came in. He told me that all the security was in place and that we were ready to proceed. I directed him to set up the courtroom. He told me that Jeanine Pirro had contacted him to ask me if she could, for her safety, remain standing in the back of the courtroom when the verdict was read, very unusual but I agreed.

I called my sergeant into the robing room and with gritted teeth asked him if we were ready to proceed. He looked at me with eyes that contained many years of courtroom experience and very quietly said, "Judge, the courtroom is packed with people whose nerves have been stretched tight for over a year and for the past six weeks at this trial. If I was the judge, who I am glad I am not, I would go out before I brought the jury out to announce the verdict and have a talk with them." I will be forever grateful for his advice. All I wanted to do was get it over with and had not thought about the spectators. I thanked him and asked him to go set up the courtroom with everyone in place except the jury.

I took a moment or two and then entered. I think I will always remember what I said to that filled courtroom.

"Ladies and gentlemen," I said, "members of the press, I want to thank you for the respect you have shown this court during a very difficult trial. The lives of two young men have been ruined. One is dead, Charles Campbell, whose son will not have a father to grow up with. Another is accused of his murder, and *his* life and career will never recover from this tragic act. I am about to bring in the jury to announce the verdict and I expect there to be no outbursts, since no one wins or loses today. It is simply a tragedy. If anyone acts out I will have you removed from the courtroom!" When I had finished my speech, you could feel a collective breath let out.

I looked at the sergeant and told him to bring the jury in.

They had deliberated for three days and you could tell from their faces that they were very glad that it was over. There is another courthouse legend that says that when the jury comes into the courtroom and they are looking at the defendant, their verdict is usually not guilty, and if they look at no one or they look at the prosecutor, that generally means a guilty verdict. These jurors were looking all over the courtroom.

After they were seated, I asked the foreperson if the jury had reached a unanimous verdict and she replied that they had. I asked her to hand the verdict sheets to the clerk who then brought them to me. I had prepared several verdict sheets for them to use, enumerating each charge against each defendant: DiGuglielmo's sheet charging him with assault, Errico's the same, and Richard D.'s sheet outlining his assault charge. I also had the sheet charging Richard D. with murder. The sheets were not handed to me in any particular order, and as I looked through them all I kept seeing was, "Not guilty," which caused me concern about the reaction of the spectators, notwithstanding the talk I had given them. I saw one sheet that said, "Guilty," but I was in such a hurry to have the verdict announced that I did not see which one it was.

As you can tell by now, we judges are not perfect people and sometimes situations get so tense that we may skip a beat in our thinking. I now had to wait as everyone else in that courtroom to hear what the jury had decided. So much for judicial privilege. I handed the sheets to the clerk who gave them back to the foreperson.

I asked her to announce the verdict and there was an audible intake of more than 100 people holding their breath. The clerk rearranged the sheets and announced that they had found Richard D., DiGuglielmo, and Errico "*not* guilty of assault." She took a big breath and then announced that they had found Richard D. "guilty of murder." There was no outburst. I thanked the jury for their service and discharged them. Reporters rushed out, and after I revoked Richard D.'s bail and ordered him to be held for sentencing, his father jumped up and yelled out, "Take me, not my son!"

At this point things got a little confusing. I do remember that when DiGuglielmo yelled at me and the spectators started standing and responding loudly, that Mike moved me very rapidly to the safe room. I really do not remember getting there nor how long I waited, but it wasn't very long until he came to get me. I remember asking him what had happened, and he told me everything was calm and that the crowd outside the courthouse had erupted in cheers when Professor McLaughlin announced the verdict – and that DA Pirro was talking to the press.

I sentenced Richard D. DiGuglielmo on December 16, 1997. I had received hundreds of letters from both the DiGuglielmo side and the Campbell supporters. The minimum sentence by statute was fifteen years to life, and the maximum was twenty-five years to life. I listened to the defendants' plea for the minimum sentence and then to Charles Campbell's thirteen-year-old son and Charles's brother address the court. Richard D. never apologized to the Campbell family for the death of their loved one.

I will tell you that I was not as happy with the verdict as I might have been. I know that I am sworn to be impartial, but I believed that DiGuglielmo should have been convicted of the assault charge. But, since judges have a sworn obligation to be fair and not let personal feelings influence their judgment, I sentenced Richard D. to twenty years to life in state prison. After pronouncing the sentence, I said, "In my opinion, it was DiGuglielmo's father who was responsible for the violence. The court is powerless to mete out punishment to the person who deserves it the most." I looked at DiGuglielmo and told him, "You acted in a manner that was mindlessly vicious and morally reprehensible!"

A week before sentencing, David Lewis had filed a 129-page motion asking me to set aside the jury verdict since I had made "inherently prejudicial" decisions in the way I had handled the notes sent to me during jury deliberations by the jury. The DA responded that I "had in fact read the notes in open court and that was a matter of record, if Mr. Lewis had any objections he should have made them then." Lewis also argued that the jury did not have sufficient proof to find Richard D. guilty. I denied the motion.

The next step was the appeal process: first, the appeal went to the Appellate Division, which affirmed the conviction, and then it went to the highest court in New York, the Court of Appeals, which refused to change the decision of the Appellate Division.

I thought that the drama had ended, but eleven years later, a Westchester County Court judge, Rory Bellantoni, decided to reverse the murder conviction. In his sixty-nine-page decision[1], Judge Bellantoni cited *The Wizard of Oz* at length to justify his reasoning. Believing that the police and the DA's office had abused their power in order to secure DiGuglielmo's conviction, he equated them to the story's titular wizard: "...No matter how scary the voice behind the curtain may seem, there is nothing to fear, as the voice behind the curtain is impotent and suffers from delusions of grandeur. For what the wizards behind the curtain fail to realize is that true power lies not in the creating of an illusion, but to do justice for all within the earshot of the wizard's voice, be they the humblest of munchkins, the most mischievous flying creatures, the most evil of witches or the most innocent of newcomers to the wizard's domain."

Knowing the case so well, my interpretation of this unusual series of references is as follows: The witness that he believed was coerced was the "innocent newcomer to the wizard's domain" (much like Dorothy Gale), and this witness was convinced by the Dobbs Ferry police to change his story in order to support the prosecution's version of events. It also seems the judge was implying that the DA's office was the "wizard behind the curtain," allowing (if not encouraging) the coercion to happen. Judge Bellantoni also blasted ADA Patricia Murphy, accusing her of hiding information about one witness from the defense; and then, believe it or not, he criticized the Court of Appeals for how they handled the case. I was about the only person he did not attack.

I cannot for the life of me understand what came over him. Professor Randolph McLaughlin told the press, "In all my years of practice, I've never seen a judge go so far out on a limb. I'd compare Judge Bellantoni's decision to *Alice In Wonderland* because it went through the looking glass. When a neutral, less

---

1 *People v DiGuglielmo,* 2008 NY Slip Op 51938(U) [21 Misc 3d 1103(A)].

emotionally involved judge looks at his decision, it'll be thrown out on its ear." I must admit that when I read the decision and thought about what went on in the judge's head, I was also reminded of *The Wizard of Oz*, specifically the Scarecrow, who sang, "If I only had a brain!"

The district attorney vowed to immediately appeal Judge Bellantoni's decision. The DA at that time was Janet DiFiore who said, "The decision is wrong on the facts and wrong on the law." The district attorney then filed an appeal from this rather startling—and in my opinion outrageous decision. It took almost two years for the appeals court to reach the case.

Twenty months after Judge Bellantoni reversed the murder conviction, it was reinstated. Four Supreme Court justices of the Appellate Division unanimously ruled that any new statements from witnesses produced by the defense would not have been enough to convince the jury to acquit the defendant. They directed that Richard D. DiGuglielmo return to prison in two days. On October 27, 2010, Richard D. DiGuglielmo was sent back to prison to complete his sentence, and Judge Bellantoni has since resigned from the bench.

I really believed that this was the very end of that case. That finally the Campbell family could count on getting the closure they wanted. Not to be so. There was *another* appeal to the federal appeals court and at long last, on September 11, 2011, the appeals court rejected Richard D. DiGuglielmo's bid to overturn his conviction. The US Court of Appeals for the Second Circuit ruled that DiGuglielmo had failed to prove that the guilty verdict would have been any different.

An end. I hope so.

24

PRACTICING LAW: "YOU'RE FROM *THE CITY,* AREN'T YOU?"

I WANT TO return to the topic of attorneys. They practice—or in some instances *practiced*—a noble profession. Thus far, I have criticized lawyers for advertising and for overcharging. I can tell you that after sitting as a trial judge and watching good, great, mediocre, and outright incompetent lawyers, I've gotten a rather jaundiced viewpoint.

After all my years in the legal profession, and after teaching at Pace Law School, I can assure you that a young law graduate is virtually worthless in the average legal practice. I was responsible for banning laptops in the courses I taught at the law school in 2008. I had observed that there was less participation in class and much less attention paid by the students in my opinion who did not seem to be just taking notes on their computers. After some complaints to the Dean and to me, the ban went into effect. After just a couple of weeks the change was obvious. The rationale I gave the students was that not only had class participation improved greatly, but also that you would not dare to have a laptop in front of you when interviewing a client or in a courtroom when conducting a trial. After one month, other professors banned laptops.

These new graduates have a lot of theoretical knowledge but little, if any, practical knowledge as to how to *practice* law. The very high-paying Wall Street firms that hire the best graduates from the top schools shove them into a library and demand that they produce at least sixty hours or more of billable time each week. They become good at research and very good at legal writing, but they still need to be trained and nursed along until they can practice independently. Other graduates either have specialized in niche law or will be hired by firms that specialize in that field and are willing to train the young cubs. Many will join a family firm, and many more will go to work for the government or public service organizations.

All new attorneys need training, and I have maintained for years that law schools must add to their curriculum courses that consist of the "nuts and bolts" of legal practice, courses that will teach them how to interview a client, how to set fees, how to dress, and how to show proper decorum in a courtroom. Think about all the training and practice the medical profession provides before setting their graduates loose on the public!

Let me tell you about my own inexperience. It was 1976, and I had finished my three years as an assistant district attorney in Brooklyn, another three in Westchester, set up my private practice in Chappaqua, and was breezing along. Up to that point I had done nothing but criminal law work and had tried cases for other attorneys. But that had meant that they had done all the preparation and had briefed me on the law for that particular case. I had just started to do civil law and was learning all about real estate law, mostly with the help of my dad, who had joined me in the Chappaqua practice.

I'd like to offer a short aside to explain how I got my dad to come to Chappaqua to practice law with my firm. Dad had been sitting as a small claims court judge in Brooklyn and had decided hundreds of cases. One evening Mom and Dad were at home when the doorbell rang, and when Dad answered the door he recognized the man as a litigant who had recently appeared before him, and who had lost his small claims case. The man started yelling at Dad and slammed the glass storm door so hard that it shattered and cut Dad's head. The injuries were not serious, but the head is so vascular that there was a lot of blood. He was taken to the hospital, treated, and eventually released.

Meanwhile, Mom had called me to ask what she should do about the attacker and I told her I would take care of it. Before I left to check on my dad that night, I called some of my old friends at the Brooklyn district attorney's office to ask for whatever help they could offer. The Honorable Elliott Golden was kind enough to tell me not to worry, that he would personally look into the case. Suffice it to say that the perpetrator was caught that night and, based on the call I got from the arresting officer, had received "street justice." (Maybe he resisted arrest?)

After that incident, Mom and Dad decided that it was time to leave Brooklyn, so I offered Dad the senior consulting attorney job in my office, even though he had officially retired. He smiled, and we both felt good about the irony of my asking him to join *my* firm, and then he accepted.

Dad taught me all about residential and commercial real estate closings, leases, cooperatives, and condominiums. My practice was thriving when I got a call from my sister Lonni, who told me that a dear friend of hers, Cindy, had been driving on an upstate country road and was hit from the rear by a pickup truck. She had hired an attorney to represent her and had just received a settlement offer. Cindy had suffered severe and crippling injuries to her arm and was not able to continue her work as an antique furniture restorer. She was a wonderfully bright, honest young woman and she and her husband were now struggling to pay their bills because she had stopped working. Cindy's lawyer told her that she had received an offer of $10,000 to settle, that Cindy would net $6,600 and the lawyer thought Cindy should take that offer. My sister felt that this was wrong and asked my opinion. It being my sister, I agreed immediately to interview Cindy and her husband free of charge.

I was immediately touched by their honesty and by the impression that they only wanted to do what was right. I asked Cindy what she hoped to get out of the case, and she said that all she wanted to do was open a flower shop in town, so that she could bring home an income to help support the family. I asked her how much she felt that would cost. She responded that they had already spoken to a florist who was retiring, and that it would cost between forty and fifty thousand for her to take over the store, with a long and favorable lease and all the inventory. They had already gone to their bank and their families and tried unsuccessfully to borrow all the funds. I told them that I would request the file from Cindy's attorney, read it over, and get back to them with my opinion.

I contacted the other attorney, sent her Cindy's written consent for me to review the file, and after much arguing and threatening on my part, she sent me the file. It was practically empty. I called her and asked if she had gone to the scene, taken photographs, and gotten the medical records, or done any investigative work at all. She replied, "Not yet." This was a year and a half after the accident.

I called Cindy and set up an appointment to visit the scene of the accident. It took over an hour and a half to drive there. I took photos and statements from Cindy and the EMT's who were at the scene, and requested copies of the police reports and Cindy's medical records. With the help and advice of my dad and my brother (who had done a considerable amount of negligence cases himself), I decided to take the case. When I told the other attorney that she had been totally negligent and did not deserve a dime, she reluctantly agreed and signed off on what's called a "substitution of attorney." I obtained all the medical records and notified all parties that I was requesting an *examination before trial* (an EBT) as soon as possible. An EBT is the device lawyers use to find out as much as they can about what the parties will testify to at trial.

The day arrived, and after another long trip upstate I conducted the EBT with the driver who had hit Cindy so hard that Cindy's car had been pushed off the road and rolled over into a ditch. The driver who had hit her could not have been nicer. She testified that she had been distracted by some deer on the side of the road and was so sorry about what had happened to Cindy. I could not have been happier for Cindy or had more going for the case: there was admitted negligence, terrible injuries—and a $250,000 insurance policy.

When I got back to my office, I called my brother and told him what had happened. He listened and then said, "I would rather be lucky than good anytime! You could not have asked for more, the case is worth a *lot* more than a ten-thousand-dollar settlement, and that first lawyer should be disbarred."

Armed with this great turn of events, I notified the court upstate that I was ready for a pre-trial conference. This is the device lawyers and courts use to try to settle cases before trial. It was mandatory to have the conference since no judge would set the case down for trial without first having a pre-trial conference.

The day arrived, and bright-eyed and bushy-tailed I sailed upstate. My brother had briefed me on how to handle the conference and offered me his opinion on how much an upstate court might think the case was worth and what I should demand.

I was about to go to a strange courthouse in a very small farming town not knowing anyone but my client. To call me *naïve* would be a compliment.

I entered the courthouse and found my client and the insurance company's lawyer and their representative. We all greeted one another cordially and waited to be called in to see the judge. The judge's secretary came out and said the judge would like to speak to the defendant's representatives first. The two of them went in, and we waited until they came out, at which time the judge said he would like to see me without my client. I went in, greeted the judge, and he said, "Hello. You're from *The City*, aren't you?" I'd heard that upstate people do not really like city people, and I knew I was in trouble right away. I blurted out, "No, Sir—north of The City. *Way* north," was my stammering response. (Chappaqua was less than an hour's drive north of Manhattan, but he didn't need to know that!)

He told me to sit down and asked me what I thought my client *might* be entitled to. As I began explaining her medical condition, he interrupted and said he had read all that. I started to explain that the first offer from the insurance company was very low and he interrupted again, saying, "Just tell me what *you* think your client ought to get out of this case."

I looked him in the eye, unaccustomed to being intimidated by a judge in this way, and said, "$250,000." He actually sputtered and turned red in the face, and then very quietly looked at me and asked, "Do you know how much a good milk cow costs?"

I have very rarely in my entire life been speechless, but I *was speechless*. I looked at him and said, "I have no idea." Apparently I *was* from the city.

He took a deep breath and said, "A good milk cow is worth about fifty thousand dollars. No case in this county with a jury of farmers has ever awarded more than fifty thousand dollars to anyone for an auto accident. Go talk to your client and I will try to get you twenty-five thousand dollars." I walked out of chambers and went to talk to Cindy. When I told her what had happened, she surprised me. She looked at me quizzically and asked me the name of the judge. When I told her, she smiled and said, "I am surprised [that the offer is so low]; the judge and my father were in Rotary Club together." Now, I felt pretty good about my knowledge of the law but did not understand what that really meant. I asked her about the judge's offer to try to get her $25,000, and she said, "You do what you think is right. I completely trust your judgment." Talk about pressure.

I went back into the judge's chambers as the attorney and insurance men walked out with grins on their faces. I looked at the judge and told him, "With due respect, Your Honor, we will take our chances at trial! But I do want to mention that my client asked me to tell you that you were a member of Rotary with her dad."

He looked at me astounded and said, "You represent little Cindy? Why didn't you tell me before? Bring the lawyer and insurance guy back in!"

I walked out immediately and told them to go see the judge. They must have thought that I had agreed to take the $25,000 offer. I sat with Cindy and we waited. A couple of minutes passed, and the insurance man rushed out to the public telephones. Fifteen minutes later, he went back in to the judge's chambers, and two minutes after that it was again my turn to see the judge.

I went in and he offered me a chair and said, "I am going to tell you what I think this case should settle for. If you and Cindy disagree that's your decision, but I think you should take it. The one-time, not-to-be-repeated offer is one hundred and twenty-four thousand dollars." I looked at him and told him that my client had authorized me to accept the offer, "but she would like to say hello to you." He said, "I will come out to greet her – but make it very short."

I am almost embarrassed to retell this event and what it took to get to where the case should have been in the first place. The settlement was just and proper, and the abuse I took for being from, "The City" and not knowing the cost of a milk cow ended up not bothering me a whit. What bothered me was the judge's attitude. I swore that if I were ever in his position (little did I know) I would never treat a lawyer like that. I never again went to a strange courthouse without doing my homework to learn who the participants were and who the judge was. No, I may not have had to learn anything more about the price of livestock, but I never made that mistake again. The Boy Scouts said it first: "Be prepared!"

My client was ecstatic, and I was made an honorary member of the family. They bought the flower shop and are still doing extremely well. On the long drive home that day, I laughed a lot, some of it for the judge, some of it for my *naïveté*.

There is so much more to learn after you pass the bar exam.

25

Making Unpopular Decisions

A few years ago, there was so much controversy surrounding the building of a mosque near Ground Zero that it sounded un-American to be in favor of it. When cool heads prevail, not political or religious extremist groups, perhaps logic will win out. Ours is a country founded on religious freedom. To racially profile and punish an entire religion because of extreme radicals who call themselves Muslims is wrong and unconstitutional.

I was faced with a similar question in 2001. The Church of Jesus Christ of Latter-day Saints wanted to build a Mormon temple in the wealthy Westchester suburb of Harrison, New York. The proposed height of the temple was higher than the local code allowed. The church needed a variance for fifteen feet, and the town had delayed granting the variance for five years. The church wanted a temple that was fifty-three feet tall, and the town wasn't willing to allow more than thirty-eight feet.

It seems like a simple question of the town granting a variance or not. The real question that arose was that the blue bloods of Harrison did not want the church at all. There was much public outcry and the usual snob statement: NIMBY (Not In *My* Backyard).

I ruled in favor of the church with a simple four-page opinion, the gist of which was, "The court in no way means to denigrate [the board's] efforts, methods, or motives in their consideration of the [Church's] application...but I caution the board against ruling in response to community opinion and not on the merits of the law." I have to tell you that if I had been the judge appointed to decide if the mosque be built near Ground Zero, I would have had to apply the law as evenhandedly as I was sworn to do, and I would have had to rule in favor of the mosque.

Here are more unfavorable things I have had to do that the public criticized me for. I am not in the least bit complaining, I did my job and have a very clear conscience, albeit it is matched with a lot of scars.

I imagine that by this time you have realized that the District Attorney's office has no love lost for any judge who rules against that office. I believe that when I issued a particular ruling against the DA's office in 1997, I may have touched a raw nerve. When the law is clear, you will be held accountable. It is my impression that the DA did not take this ruling well, notwithstanding the law.

The case was a bit complex. The District Attorney had subpoenaed a lawyer's records (using a grand jury subpoena) from a neutral attorney who had been appointed to safeguard the files of this attorney. The attorney was under suspicion of some wrongdoing prior to this time, and turned over the files as ordered by the subpoena. The DA used material from those records in prosecuting the lawyer.

The issues were simple: Did the District Attorney's office issue a grand jury subpoena before there was a grand jury investigating the person, and before there was a criminal proceeding pending (as the law stated was necessary)? After reviewing the record, I ruled that the District Attorney's office lacked the authority to issue any subpoena or use the material it received in any future case. In my decision, I used such terms as "greatly disturbed," and the "questionable practices" regarding the prosecutor's office.

I guess that whenever you hand down a decision that finds the possibility of prosecutorial misconduct, you are not going to make friends in the District Attorney's office. Remember what I mentioned earlier in this book—the grand jury can be a prosecutor's "plaything." It is clear that there must be a system of checks and balances. No one can have so much power without there being a watchdog, or someone with that power might abuse the system.

In addition to judges, lawyers (whether they are defense attorneys or prosecutors) also have the potential to overstep the legitimate bounds of their authority. In this book I have tried to point out how judges have to balance the scales so that no abuse takes place. Decisions have to be made according to the law. We must follow the right path or our laws mean nothing. I have tried to do that my entire career. Perhaps it was a little easier for me since I was elected to the bench after I had a very successful law practice. I was in the unique position of not owing anything to anyone (except perhaps the Cuban-American Caucus of Port Chester). I was free to look at every case based only on its own merits. I am sad to say that that may not always be the case for every judge. I am not talking about anything as overt as bribery or corruption, but the subtle pressure that some judges feel because they have received large campaign donations from some law firm, or they have to worry about being reelected and do not want to step on the wrong toes. Even justices of our US Supreme Court have accepted paid trips from law firms, which is not in violation of the ethics that bind the Supreme Court justices, but might in some people's opinion exert some subtle undue influence on the justices.

Having said all that, I am reminded of a case that I decided as an acting justice for the Orange County, NY Supreme Court. Judge Joseph A. Owen had ruled in favor of the County, and the case was appealed to me. The issue at hand was a huge building project planned for renovation as well as plans to build a new jail in the county. Approving the county's project labor agreement was supposed to be a slam-dunk, but it turned out to be a very difficult legal issue. The then-administrative judge Angelo Ingrassia assigned the case to me. I am sure that no other judge wanted to handle this hot potato, and it is my sincere belief by now that Judge Ingrassia did either love me or hated me since I seemed to end up with an inordinate amount of hard cases.

Here comes another group of people that I have yet to criticize: labor unions. Please do not misinterpret what I have to say. I am not anti-union, not at all. But I am against certain practices that force decisions to be made that I consider contrary to the public good.

Orange County had reached an agreement calling for the use of a predominantly union workforce (known as a PLA) to build and renovate the new prison. While there is nothing wrong with the agreement to use predominantly union labor, the county did not go through the county's customary use of competitive bidding, according to the New York State statutes governing such agreements. The county's excuse for not doing so was that it was merely avoiding labor strife by agreeing to the PLA without going through the usual channels.

I voided the contract as being violative of the law. There was no showing of "dire need" to use this method of agreement to avoid a labor work stoppage. I stated in part that, "[A] determination to use a project labor agreement (PLA) in order to avoid the costs associated with such activity, which resulted in incidents of disruptive, possibly illegal, union activity which had been perpetrated in response to the use of nonunion personnel on other projects, smacks of capitulation to extortion." I handed down that decision in April of 1997, which was the time that I stopped being invited by the administrative judge to join the other judges for lunch in their private lunchroom. Hmmm.

When Orange County appealed my ruling, they challenged it on the basis that I had, in the opinion, given credit to a law school intern who had helped research the law of the case, a summer intern from law school who worked with my principal law clerk to help with legal research. The final line of my decision against the County of Orange was: "The court wishes to acknowledge the invaluable assistance of Ms. Joy Farber, Pace University School of Law, in the preparation of this decision." To quote the reporter, one of the few I respect and who did his homework and researched the issue, "It's a courtesy: recognizing a law school intern's work so she can put it on her resume."

The county pounced on the line and tried to use it as leverage to have me quit the case and turn it over to a new judge, because Pace Law School runs the Pace Environmental Litigation Clinic, which helped represent Riverkeeper in a controversial, continuing lawsuit over the county's failed $52 million dump expansion. The county attorney went on to say that it is a conflict for me to have *relied* on Farber since she *must* have a personal vested interest in Riverkeeper recovering its legal fees from Orange County (since Pace would benefit from such an outcome). The attorney went on to say that Farber's relationship with the lawsuit "causes one to reasonably question the impartiality" of her help in the case, even though she had no direct relationship with the lawsuit. I often have wondered if that attorney could look himself straight in the face when he wrote that.

You can only imagine the reaction to my ruling. Suffice it to say that my decision did not endear me to the unions, Orange County, or the administrative judge, who, as my luck would have it, lived in Orange County. The Appellate Division reversed my ruling. I am reminded that "The two things you do not want to watch being made are sausage and the law." By the way, this definitely includes legislatures writing laws around midnight when everyone is too tired to think clearly.

I find it curious that immediately following this case, I was assigned to do a mental health hearing. These occur when someone petitions the court to be released from a mental health facility, claiming that they have recovered from their infirmity and should be returned to the public domain. I am not saying I was being punished, but these are not the type of cases I was doing and I had never had any training in these types of proceedings. Nevertheless, I proceeded to set the hearing down in my calendar and I hoped that I could adequately prepare for it.

The petitioner appeared before me with an attorney, and the state's council was there representing the people. One of the witnesses was a psychiatrist from the hospital who testified that it was their recommendation that the petitioner *not* be released at this time, but who also admitted that he was not her treating doctor.

The petitioner's attorney asked me if the petitioner could respond to the doctor's testimony and agree to be cross-examined afterward. I agreed, and this middle-aged, well-dressed, attractive woman took the stand. She testified at length that she was aware of her problems – she had attempted suicide and struck her daughter in anger – but that Dr. Freud (her treating psychiatrist; fictitious name, of course) had been of great help in her realizing how wrong she had been and had helped her face her infirmity over the past four years. She was also aware that while her treating psychiatrist did not think she was fully ready to return to society, she felt she was.

The state attorney politely suggested that I ask the woman a few questions about what she would do if I released her. He had a small, funny grin on his face.

With some *naiveté* I asked her a few simple questions and then asked her what would she do when she left the hospital if I granted her petition? She looked at me and with a sincere voice said, "I will go home and tell my daughter how sorry I am for my prior conduct. I will then find out where Dr. Freud lives and go to his house as soon as I can, take a knife with me and cut his balls off!" Suffice it to say, I denied her petition and asked the administrative judge not to assign me to any more mental health hearings.

Generally speaking, judges are neither too hard nor too lenient. We are faced with so many situations that call for individual justice in each case, that our rulings and decisions contain a broad spectrum of decisions. The media tries to label judges, and my dislike for such labeling is monumental. I have three scrapbooks of press clippings reporting on the cases I have tried and decisions I have written. I have never had a reporter study how many of my cases would be considered "tough but fair," how many were "too lenient," or any other measure of what I was really like as a judge. I also have never seen them interview any other judge to determine the same facts. I know "sex and violence" sells papers. I am also aware that extremes of all sorts sell papers.

I once sentenced a career burglar to 125-years-to-life in prison and the media wrote all about it. I was quoted as "scolding" the defendant when, during sentencing, I told him, "You've had your run. I plan to put a stop to it. The criminal justice system has failed by allowing you to be at liberty as long as you have." I then pointed out to him that his favorite targets were the homes of elderly people, mostly widows and widowers.

"Sometimes, all they have left of the life and family they once knew is their home and its contents. You step in and take the last of what they have—a treasured heirloom, a husband's watch, a deceased wife's wedding ring."

You might ask me why I was so disturbed by this criminal. Another of the few reporters that I respect, Bruce Golding of the *Gannett Suburban Newspapers*, picked up the story and reported that Mr. Bunker "stole a child's jar of coins and carried it off in the boy's *Power Rangers* knapsack." Bunker had been arrested at the White Plains railroad station on the day of the burglary still carrying the *Power Rangers* knapsack containing the broken glass jar, $185 in coins, jewelry, and a gold watch he had stolen in an earlier burglary. As hard as a judge tries to remain impartial, there are times when a criminal steps across a line that should not be crossed and a judge decides that it is time to deal with them in an appropriate manner. When a jury convicted Bunker of five counts of felony burglary, I enthusiastically gave him the maximum sentence allowed by law.

I received some more criticism for the following case, but by this time I was so used to it that this one really didn't bother me. I had found a circus performer guilty of a lesser charge than the one the public wanted, a man by the name of Norman Kaldaev, who worked for Circus with a Purpose, a circus that uses neglected or abandoned animals in its performances to teach children about the environment, animal cruelty, and respect for the planet. Norman was a horseman with the troupe.

The testimony and police reports revealed that after a performance, Norman was invited to join five people on an early morning cruise on the Hudson River. The group apparently consumed a great deal of alcohol on the cruise. The wife went to rest in a stateroom and, while it is unclear whether or not she invited Norman to join her, the next thing we know is that the husband walked into the stateroom and saw Norman, fully clothed (as was the wife), lying on the bed on top of the man's wife. He and the other guests proceeded to beat Norman to a pulp.

Norman was a native of Kazakhstan and his command of the English language may have been inadequate, since he claimed through his attorney that he was "accidentally tossed on top of the woman by a wave that rocked the boat." The woman testified that the boat had returned to the dock in Ossining, NY and was tied up when the incident happened, that Norman was an uninvited intruder. She insisted that Norman be charged with burglary and sexual abuse.

I tried the case nonjury and it was obvious that the boat people had invited him on the boat, but nothing else was obvious. I dismissed all the charges except for the far lesser misdemeanor charge of sexual abuse in the third degree, a molestation charge. It was hard to give much credibility to the wife's testimony since she had no injuries or bruising, was at all times fully clothed and was completely intoxicated, nor to Norman, who should probably not have gone to her stateroom but whose overall conduct I did not find particularly egregious. He had, in fact, been beaten bloody and subsequently lost his job with the circus.

In trying to resolve the case, I found that Norman had just barely stepped across the line and the sentence reflected the verdict, a six-month conditional discharge.

My decision was not well received by the boat owners, who sent me nasty letters after the sentencing, letters that made me realize that not one of them took any responsibility for any of their actions. Methinks the lady doth protest too much. Likewise, my decision was not appreciated by the district attorney's office, which had sent ADA Frederick Green to address the court, calling upon me to impose the maximum sentence of jail time on Norman because he had denied any wrongdoing during a pre-sentence interview with the Westchester County Probation Department. Now, I happen to like Fred Green and I do not know if he received his orders from his boss, but could we draw the line somewhere and stop pandering to the public?

26

Halting the Abuse of Power

It would be an easy thing to say that sentencing a defendant puts an end to a case, but in reality a judge does not leave cases like these in the courthouse. I do not know of any judge who can completely turn off the sights and sounds that reveal man's inhumanity to man—and women. We cannot close our minds to the things we see and the things we hear. Yet, for all the horrible and devastating stories, there were also many times that a touch of courage or a spark of humanity would shine brightly in a case. I juggled a myriad of emotions in the courtroom.

You'll remember that I have no complaints. I loved my job. When I watch the news and see and hear about a really heinous case that has happened somewhere, I think out loud that I would *love* to be sitting in judgment of that person. I imagine sitting in judgment of Bernie Madoff, O. J. Simpson, or Lindsay Lohan. Now *there*'s a girl who'd have received her share of judicial wisdom from me! But then I remember that I was privileged to sit on so many important cases, and that I had made my best effort to see to it that justice was done.

By this time you must realize that no one, large or small, was an intimidating factor when it came to my making the right decision. It would be absurdly pompous to say that I always reached the right decision. I didn't. But in the eighteen years that I sat on the bench, I was reversed only three times out of the thousands of cases I presided over. (I guess that the Appeals Courts weren't ready to change the status quo for those cases). I had great principal law clerks and researchers, and I had the will to fight the good fight. I had the best role models possible in my parents, who always taught us to protect the people that needed protection and help the ones who needed help. To give back in life makes it worth the junk you sometime have to put up with.

To have your picture and decision published on the front page of the *New York Law Journal* (March 16, 1999) is prestigious enough, but to know that once again you have stopped someone with a lot of power from abusing that power is better.

That case started when the City of New York informed communities in Westchester County (who drew water from the New York City-owned network of aqueducts from Upstate New York), that they planned to shut down the Croton Aqueduct from mid-July to mid-September. The city based their argument on permits they had issued to water companies to allow them to draw water from the New York City supply. The city also sought a declaration of their rights under 1937 permits issued by the City of New York to New Rochelle stating that New York City would not be liable for any damage that inhabitants of the respective communities suffered by an interruption or shutoff of the flow of water for an inspection of or repairs to the system. The New Rochelle and Briarcliff Manor communities argued that the summer months were the peak draw time for water, and that such action by the City of New York would pose a health risk to the public. After a lot of negotiations, the parties reached a tentative compromise solution: deliver *less* water during that period of time, instead of no water.

Taking on a contract that was written fifty-two years ago, 1937, was an easy contract law question. Was it a contract that protected the public? Was it fair when written? These and many other questions had to be answered. My opinion stated in part, "To the extent that the contracts vest such unfettered discretion in [the City], the City's option to unilaterally discontinue delivery of potable water to petitioners is invalid and unenforceable." I reasoned, "Courts will not enforce or compel the specific performance of a contract where the performance compelled thereby will bring about a result which is detrimental to the public interest. The amount of water that petitioners can draw from alternate sources—particularly during a peak demand period—is limited, as are their storage capacities. There is, therefore, a substantial possibility that a prolonged shutdown of the Croton Aqueduct during such a peak demand period could pose severe health and safety risks for the communities which petitioners serve."

The *Law Journal* headline read "CITY MUST KEEP WATER FLOWING." This really was an easy case for me. And you see, judges protect the public even when the public knows very little about it.

27

Bonnie Briar Syndicate vs. the Town of Mamaroneck

Since there were so many controversial cases to write about, I tried to pick a few that you would find the most interesting. I have been tough when it was called for in my opinion and lenient when I thought I might be able to turn someone's life around. I have taken on towns and cities. I have decided for and against police departments and district attorneys. I have sided with criminal defendants when the law gave me no choice. I have helped create new laws and I have helped teach these principles to many others.

Now, I want to tell you about one last very controversial case. Bonnie Briar is a country club in Mamaroneck, New York, in use as a country club continuously since 1921. In 1996, the owners of the club wanted to build seventy-one homes around the course, re-routing the layout of the golf course in the process. The town of Mamaroneck was adamantly opposed to any more building and enacted legislation to block this project, particularly when several studies found that the land contained wetlands and scenic vistas, was within the critical flood plain of the town, and was situated on Long Island Sound, which is well known to have innumerable environmental problems of its own.

The town re-zoned the country club property from single-family homes to a recreational zoning district, thereby stopping any development of housing on the property. This is known as taking action *ex post facto*, or after the fact, and Bonnie Briar Syndicate (the Syndicate runs the country club) claimed that the town's actions were an unconstitutional taking of its property.

After much research, case review, and discussion, Al Degatano, my first law clerk, came into my chambers and asked what decision I would render. He looked flabbergasted when I told him, and he said he did not think the decision would be good enough to withstand an appeal. Nevertheless, we drafted the opinion and after several rewrites, I handed it down. The case was appealed and I was affirmed all the way up to the US Supreme Court, who refused to hear the case (in other words, letting my decision stand).

This would seem to be a case that few people would get excited about, but how wrong that turned out to be! My ruling recognized *not* municipalities' right to take property but that the best interests of the general public must prevail. I did this so that villages, towns, and cities should not assume it had become an easy matter to simply rezone at will. While I had antagonized the developers and their attorneys, I made friends of golfers all over the county who found out that I was the judge who preserved Bonnie Briar. Little did they know (or care) that it was less a decision to preserve a golf course than a defense of a town overwhelmed with overbuilding and numerous environmental challenges.

28

Good-Byes

So, I HAVE told you of the wonderful and rewarding life I have led. Most of it was indeed wonderful, but one cannot forget the moments of tragedy and grief that also shaped my persona.

With the passage of years, it is inevitable that I have lost many of those wonderful people I told you about.

In the mid 1950s, my brother Dik served in the air force for two years as a JAG officer stationed in Japan at Tachikawa Air Force Base. Since public sentiment in Japan was still very anti-American (after all, it had only been eleven years since the bombings at Hiroshima and Nagasaki), my brother spent an inordinate amount of time on-base at the officers' club, where very good Scotch was only a dollar a bottle. He became an alcoholic. Dik may have been a happy drunk, but no one really likes drunks, happy or not. By 1980, he had ruined two marriages as well as his physical being. As I've told you, we lost Dik to a heart attack when he was forty-eight years old.

I had received the call, called my sister Lonni, and together we proceeded to my parents' home to break the news to them. My father was in disbelief and my mom collapsed on the front steps. I think that was the moment she lost her spirit. Taffy and

I would have my parents over for dinner as often as possible, and my mom would get a kick out of my efforts to cook (thankfully, Taffy was a terrific cook). Eventually, my mom would come over early to help cook dinner for the family. She loved all her grandchildren and I know she had a special love for my two daughters. It was they and their cousin Tamara, Lonni's daughter, who brought her back to caring about life again.

It may be hard to imagine, but I swear that the light in Mom's eyes dimmed that day and never came back. She may have said I was her favorite, but Dik was her firstborn. They had a bond no one can fully understand unless you are a mother and you lose your firstborn child. Lonni, Taffy and I worked hard after his death to try to help her, but the battle back to caring is a very slow and uphill one.

I have already told you that Dad died after he saw me sworn in. He had suffered a severe stroke in the spring right after I was nominated to run for judge. With the help of my brother-in-law, Dr. Stanley Mirsky, we were able to get Dad into Burke Rehabilitation Hospital. He stayed there as long as they would allow, making very little progress. Soon the doctors at Burke told my mom that he'd have to have his leg amputated since it had turned gangrenous. Mom told me she could not bear to be the one to tell him, so I went to Burke, spoke to his doctors, and then went in to see him.

His speech had returned a bit, and we spoke for a while, and then I told him what the doctors had said – that he needed the operation to save his life. He looked at me, grabbed my hand in his, and said, "Please don't let them take my car away. It will make me feel more helpless than I feel now!" I excused myself for a minute, mumbling something to Dad about talking to the doctors again, and went into a waiting room to cry. Telling the doctors to go ahead with the surgery and waiting with him in the pre-op was probably one of the hardest things I have ever had to do, and before long he left our lives.

I was fifty-three, and since now the family could not go to Dad for advice, Lonni pronounced me the elder. I will confess that I did not want to *be* the elder, but realized that, as usual with Lonni, it was not a question of choice—not *my* choice, anyway. But she was right yet again, because from that day on all the relatives came to me with their problems and questions. I know that Dad's death had a profound effect on my life and my decision-making. I have always stopped to ask myself what advice he would have given me and to thank him for all the things he had taught me.

By 1999 my feisty mom had shrunk to four foot nine and weighed less than ninety pounds. She confided in me that she really did not want to see the millennium without Dad, and she died at home on August 1, two days before her ninety-first birthday.

In recent years I have tried to find out what happened to my mother's family. I have tried many websites and search engines, taken two trips to Budapest, Hungary, my mother's hometown, and twice visited the Auschwitz-Birkenau concentration camp sites in Poland in search of records of her family. I have visited the places she told me she remembered her mother talking about—Budapest's Great Synagogue on Dohány Street, the Hungarian State Opera House on Andrássy Avenue, the Matthias Church in the heart of Buda's Castle District—and walked the streets that I imagined her family members walked on. I have framed eleven postcards that were written to my grandmother Minnie during the early 1900s. They feature beautiful Elizabethan women pictured on one side and the written portion on the other. I have had the Hungarian translated, but they give no clue as to any of the relatives' whereabouts or history. I have visited whatever places were available to me in Budapest that had any records to search, but all I have ever found were some headstones with the family name and symbols engraved on them. But these were pre-Holocaust, since the Jewish people were not buried in cemeteries with headstones after the Nazis came. I guess that I will never know. I think my thoughts of who they were will center around my wonderful Grandmother Minnie and her personality, and that's how I will imagine them all.

When I lost her I felt really alone. That part of me that was always able to speak to my elders was gone. I cried a lot, but had my family for support and they were able to be there for me, in ways I only found out about when I was in that dark place. Patience, caring, unquestioning love. You survive and I do not believe that it gets easier easily. It only gets easier after an awful lot of healing.

One year and eight days after my mother died, after an eleven-month fight, the light, heart, and essence of me lost her battle, and Taffy died of cancer. Devastated, I did not know how to cope. I leaned heavily on my two girls, especially Karen. I could not work. I could not live in the house that we had shared for three decades. I could not deal with anyone. The administrative judge told me to come back to work when I felt I was ready, but I thought I would never be ready to try cases again.

I told you that I was instrumental in getting my dear sister Lonni clearance and credentials with the Red Cross to be a volunteer at Ground Zero in 2001. She served in places the EPA (Environmental Protection Agency) told us were safe, but within a few years she contracted lung cancer, and I lost that dear, huggable, lovable, naughty sister of mine to lung cancer in 2005. Lonni loved life—at times too much and admitted to me, after she fell ill, that she had crossed the line a few times, but that she regretted almost nothing she had done. Before he died, my brother Dik and I had tried as hard as we could to warn her about some of the decisions she had made, but she was a lovably stubborn person. She may have been my baby sister, but she was always a strong shoulder when I needed one.

On a bright note, I now have Bobbie Eden in my life. She has become my support and my best encouraging presence. She gently pushed me to finally sit down and get started writing this book. She has proven to me that you can fall in love a second time. Bobbie also watches the evening news with me and has to listen to all the slings and arrows I hurl at the news media and the police and detective shows.

But sadly, there is no one left from those generations of my family to tell good news or bad to, to buy presents for, to see on the holidays. I thought at first that I'd never understand why I was chosen to survive, but I'd made a promise to myself that they would never be forgotten. I wrote this book in large part to honor them. Thank you for letting me share them with you.

29

Closing Arguments

I hope that by this time I have convinced you that judges are simply people trying on a daily basis to do what's right, stand up to people or organizations that misuse their power, and see to it that the little guy—and on occasion the big guy—is protected. I hope that when you watch the news on television from now on you will take a minute to think about the other side of the story, before you fall into lockstep with the media when they damn the actions of a judge. Perhaps when you read about someone accused of violating the law you could step back and say honestly to yourself, "What would I do if I were the judge in the case?"

I've pointed out what I believe constitute the errors, omissions, and other mistakes committed by district attorneys in the name of prosecuting the guilty, and I want the reader to know that I feel the same way about any person in power who abuses his or her authority or uses it for political gain or to stroke his or her ego. I know that I keep saying that this book is not designed to simply attack the people in power who misuse that authority, but I am sure that there are judges throughout the country who are reading this and nodding their heads in agreement.

Some of my close friends have been kind enough to refer to me as "the Don Quixote of the judiciary." Yes, I admit I tilted at my share of windmills. I truly believed that it is the duty of a judge to look at the present state of the law and to decide cases based not merely on their merits but on *doing substantial justice*.

I have laid out for you everything that I believe in and the manner in which I conducted myself throughout my career. I do hope you will examine what I have said, whether or not you agree with me. If not for a check-and-balance system to control both police who sometimes overstep their bounds and prosecutors who do the same, we would be left with a chaotic set of rules. There is a need for a strong judiciary and there is an equal need to review their decisions.

Whenever I give lectures, something I have loved doing since retirement (other than writing this book), I have people come up to me afterward and offer me their opinions about everything. They unfailingly say such things as, "I believe in the death penalty!" "I am opposed to the death penalty because of the mistakes that have been made!" "Why does it take ten to twenty years of appeals for a death penalty case?" "Will Sirhan Sirhan or Charles Manson ever get out of jail?" I love these questions because they spark debate. And I am always surprised that these people think that I have all the answers to their questions. I don't. All I really want you to do is *think*. That's easy to say, I know. Perhaps I should say I want you to *question*. I think that the demand for twenty-four-hour-a-day news has caused many editors to jump to conclusions without having all the facts, thereby misleading the public to believe issues can be boiled down to quick sound bites. I am not sure if it is intentional, but I am certain it is wrong.

Tonight when you are watching the news or reading it on your computer, please take a moment to ask yourself even one question about one legal case. I guarantee you will have one to ask. And to think, “What would I do?” No matter what side of the bench you are on, whether you are a lawyer, judge, complainant, defendant, witness, or juror, we all have an awesome responsibility to make sure that the scales are equally balanced, and that the law is applied to everyone even-handedly.

About The Author

Judge Leavitt attended New York University for his Bachelor's degree and his father's alma mater, Fordham Law School, for his Juris Doctor. He spent three years in the Brooklyn District Attorney's office, another three years as an assistant DA in the Westchester County District Attorney's office, eighteen years in private practice as a defense attorney, ten years as a Town Judge, and eight years as a County Court and Acting Supreme Court justice for Westchester County, New York. He also taught as an adjunct professor of law at Pace Law School in New York.

Leavitt served for ten years in the Chappaqua Volunteer Fire Department and retired as a captain. There, he was injured in a house fire and his daughters thought he should find something safer, so he became a certified Emergency Medical Technician (which required 128 hours of instruction and testing to be certified) with the New Castle Volunteer Ambulance Corps. He served in that capacity for ten years.

The Judge served in the army and was stationed at Fort Dix, New Jersey, and then at Fort Leavenworth, Kansas. He also joined the New York Guard years later and stayed active until 2005. He was stationed at Camp Smith and retired as a lieutenant colonel.

Judge Leavitt received a medal from the New York Guard for his efforts during Hurricane Floyd, when he and his colleague Andy Freundlich drove the only Red Cross vehicle able to reach more than 150 people stranded by floodwaters at a high school in Briarcliff Manor, New York. They treated, housed, fed, and cared for them until they could arrange for transportation home. After his retirement, he continued his active involvement with the Red Cross in Florida and became a hurricane shelter chairman for the northern sector of Palm Beach County, opening shelters during storms and on one occasion housing more than seven hundred people in a middle school for over four days. Leavitt also worked with and served displaced and orphaned children from Pleasantville Cottage School for more than twenty-five years.

Throughout his career, Leavitt has served on numerous boards of directors and charities. He still remembers his mother telling him and his siblings, as soon as they could understand the real meaning of her words, "Don't be a *schnurrer* [a taker] in life. Give back!" When each of them was old enough, she would take them along to her volunteer job at a hospital, at the time referred to as a hospital for incurably sick children. At Hanukkah and Christmas, Leavitt and his siblings were told to give one of their new toys to a patient. It may not sound like a big deal, but he believes that is how to teach your children values, and he passed these lessons on to his daughters.

In telling you about his background and experiences over the years, Judge Leavitt hopes readers will gain perspective into his thinking and decision-making on matters of law, and the life experiences that shaped these decisions. When you hear the term *activist judge*, he will have given you a different slant on what that means.

For more information about author, please visit:
www.FromTheOtherSideOfTheBench.com

Made in the USA
Middletown, DE
13 March 2023